D0875754

940.4144 SHERWOOD
Sherwood, Elmer W.
A soldier in World War I : t
M   386012   04/17/12
NAFC PUBLIC LIBRARY.
New Albany-Floyd Co. Library

A Soldier in World War I

THE DIARY OF ELMER W. SHERWOOD

INDIANA HISTORICAL SOCIETY PRESS
INDIANAPOLIS 2004

A Soldier in World War I

THE DIARY OF ELMER W. SHERWOOD

edited by ROBERT H. FERRELL

© 2004 Indiana Historical Society Press. All rights reserved.

Printed in the United States of America

This book is a publication of the
Indiana Historical Society Press
450 West Ohio Street
Indianapolis, Indiana 46202-3269 USA
www.indianahistory.org
Telephone orders 1-800-447-1830
Fax orders 317-234-0562
Orders by E-mail shop.indianahistory.org

The paper in this publication meets the minimum requirements of American National Standard for Information Sciences—Permanence of Paper for Printed Library Materials, ANSI Z39.48-1984. ∞

Library of Congress Cataloging-Publication Data

Sherwood, Elmer W.
    A soldier in World War I : the diary of Elmer W. Sherwood / edited by Robert H. Ferrell.
    p.   cm.
    Includes bibliographical references and index.
    ISBN 0-87195-173-8 (alk. paper)
    1. Sherwood, Elmer W.—Diaries. 2. United States. Army. Field Artillery Regiment, 150th. 3. United States. Army—Officers—Diaries. 4. World War, 1914-1918—Personal narratives, American. 5. World War, 1914-1918—Campaigns—France. 6. World War, 1914-1918—Regimental histories—United States. I. Ferrell, Robert H. II. Title.

D570.32150th .S53 2004
940.4′144′092—dc22

                                                    2003069168

No part of this publication may be reproduced, stored in or introduced into a retrieval system, or transmitted, in any form or by any means (electronic, mechanical, photocopying, recording, or otherwise), without the prior written permission of the copyright owner.

Table of Contents

Introduction

WORLD WAR I HAD A PROFOUND AND PERMANENT EFFECT ON OUR father's life. He was so grateful to have been spared that he was cheerful, happy, and optimistic always. "You owe it to the world to be happy," he frequently said.

Unlike Erich Maria Remarque and Ernest Hemingway, who wrote about the troubles caused by World War I, our father suffered no concerns of that sort. He was ever patriotic and anxious to serve his country. He did so in the Army Reserve and as a major in World War II. In civil life he was active in community affairs, the American Legion, and Republican politics. He was enthusiastic in all of his activities and unfailingly kind and considerate in his dealings with others. He never held a grudge even though in our opinion there were times when he had a perfect right to do so. Our father enjoyed life to the fullest and was engrossed in plans for the future on the day of his death. We are so fortunate to have had such a model for our own lives.

Joan Sherwood Voyles
Robert Elmer Sherwood

Preface to *Rainbow Hoosier*

(INDIANAPOLIS: PRINTING ARTS, 1919)

HERE IS SOMETHING BETTER THAN FICTION ABOUT SOLDIERING; IT'S A soldier's straightforward writing, and line after line of it "tells more than it knows it tells." That is to say, the texture of the writing is continually illuminated by bits of narrative common-place to the author of them, but extraordinary to the delving reader. And yet, of course, the young soldier realizes all the time that he is passing through the great experience of his life; that it is an experience not to be matched by any adventure of his father or of his sons or his grandsons. He knows that his sons and grandsons will read his story; he is assured of that—not because he believes the story reveals a greatness of his own spirit, but because he knows his story is a part of American history.

—Booth Tarkington

Foreword to *Diary of a Rainbow Veteran: Written at the Front*

(TERRE HAUTE, IND.: MOORE-LANGEN, 1929)

CORPORAL SHERWOOD'S DIARY WILL RECALL TO EVERY MEMBER OF THE Rainbow Division the career of that Division in the Great War. He has recorded simply and vividly his experiences and impressions through the days of campaigns and battle. It is a story of real men, of whom he was a worthy comrade. It is characteristic of the Division that there are no belittling grumblings or criticisms in the daily thoughts of the writer. On the contrary, his record, like his conduct is pitched on a high plane of courage, service, and sacrifice. The soldier's sense of humor is mingled with pathos and the tragedy of suffering and death of loved comrades. Even the faithful horses and the almost human guns receive their full share of credit and affection. He graphically describes the marching, the fatigue, the effect of the enemy's fire, the excellence of the Division's gunnery, the matchless barrage that it helped to deliver and the fortitude and high morale with which the Division bore itself in adversity as well as in victory. Yet he does so, unconscious of conveying these impressions to his readers.

It will awaken memories in the members of the Division and it will thrill with pride those who, while not sharing its fortunes, followed it in their hearts as the representative of their Country and their States in the Great Adventure.

It was my privilege to share in organizing the 67th Field Artillery Brigade, to command the Brigade until near the end of its training, to witness the superb fighting of the Rainbow Division by my side in the St. Mihiel offensive, and to command the Fifth Corps, when it again came under my command in the great offensive of the Meuse-Argonne. Everywhere the Division gave proof of the finest fighting spirit and once when our infantry was sorely depleted by losses, the gallant artillery commanders offered to spare some of their cannoneers who were armed with the rifle to give temporary relief.

This Diary will interpret to our people the spirit of the men whom they sent to battle. As a tale of adventure it will fascinate

the reader and it will not fail to be an incentive to all who admire brave
deeds and nobility of soul.

—Charles P. Summerall
General, Chief of Staff
United States Army

Preface to *A Soldier in World War I: The Diary of Elmer W. Sherwood*

HERE IS A HOOSIER CLASSIC, A DIARY ACCOUNT THAT WILL LAST AND not be overwhelmed by other books about either its author's era or later times. It is a simply wonderful drawing, a veritable photograph one might say, of what it was like to go through a great war. This is a narrative of a youth who volunteered to serve his country in April 1917 and before long found himself in France living a hard life, and a dangerous one, in an artillery regiment of the 42nd (Rainbow) Division.

Elmer Sherwood was an observer with uncommonly good judgment. If his descriptions lacked perfection they partook of an attractive innocence that brought out the truth. If he became grandiloquent, lyrical, he soon retired from his perch and recorded what lay closer in view. Withal he showed the humor of moments, if he could discern any, so that he did not produce in his diary a series of complaints about living in dugouts that were little more than holes, or about the food that was so distasteful with its cornwillie (corned beef), slumgullion (stew of an uncertain origin), and hardtack (which was what it sounded like). Nor did he complain unduly of the mud and rain of autumnal France when his division came into the greatest battle in all of American history, the Meuse-Argonne, for men were dying everywhere—the Argonne cost 26,000 lives, one in five of its casualties of 120,000, the latter one in ten of the 1.2 million soldiers who entered that dreadful place. He was, suitably, thankful to be alive.

Sherwood published two books about his experiences, but each of these accounts in their individual ways did not do those experiences justice. The first book was a narrative, without the diary, and therefore lacked the immediacy of events. The second, which its author described as his diary, contained only part of it, and that portion he brushed up, prettified, and occasionally added passages, so that the diary entries as published were not, as he related, "written at the front."

The present book includes all of the diary that has survived, notably experiences in the army of occupation that among other things saw the Rainbow Hoosier, as he described himself, taking an unauthorized trip to Paris, this because a pretty black-haired girl from Chicago, working in a Red Cross canteen, challenged him to do so. All the entries, moreover, are as he wrote them; a reader easily understands what he meant, even if he skipped a word or missed the plural of a verb or committed some egregious misspelling (he was quite capable of the last). The entries as they now stand indeed were written at the front.

One section of the diary does not appear, and it is impossible to include, for he lost it sometime after publication of the narrative book of years ago. He kept a diary from the beginning of his service until February 1918, a diary book he mentioned when he commenced a new one in the latter month. For this period it has been necessary to use the narrative in *Rainbow Hoosier* (1919). The present text does include a shipboard diary he sent home from France shortly after arrival, which appeared in his home-town newspaper.

There is an aspect of nostalgia about Sherwood's diary that deserves mention as this book goes to press. The surviving veterans of World War I within the State of Indiana now number a bare half-dozen, all of them aged one hundred or more. The marching millions of the war of long ago, 1917–18, four million of them, are almost entirely gone. Memory of them, one must hope, will survive because of what they wrote about their time.

Elmer W. Sherwood was born in Linton, Indiana, sixty miles as the crow flies from Indianapolis, in 1896, and as a youth listened to the Civil War stories of his grandfather who had been away from home for three years, and often heard his grandmother tell of her loneliness as she awaited her husband's return. He marched proudly as a flag bearer in Linton's GAR parades in honor of Memorial Day and of July 4, the town's largest annual events. After high school he enrolled at Indiana University in nearby Bloomington, where he majored in English. When war came, and prompted by his grandfather's service, he enlisted, joining the National Guard unit in Indianapolis that became the 150th Field Artillery Regiment.

After the war he returned to the university—he had been a sophomore when he enlisted. He reported for the campus newspaper, the *Indiana Daily Student*, for which he wrote a column, "Familiar Stories about Familiar Students." Thereafter he moved in several directions. While still at the university he was elected to the state legislature and served in the Indiana House of Representatives in the 1921–22 session, where he sponsored bills creating the Indiana World War Memorial plaza and the American Legion national headquarters in Indianapolis. He was clerk of Greene County from 1922 to 1935. He taught English at Linton High School, assisted the Sherwood (no relation) Templeton Coal Company and the Central Indiana Coal Company with public relations, and in the latter 1930s was editor of the *National Legionnaire*, the official publication of the American Legion.

During World War II he again served his country as an officer in the U.S. Army and was director of public relations at Fort Harrison, the army's huge installation in northeast Indianapolis.

The late 1940s and the 1950s proved the most active period in his life. He formed Sherwood Associates, a public relations firm, in Indianapolis, retained his keen interest in American Legion affairs, and became prominent politically as a leading Republican in his state. He was an early supporter of Gen. Dwight D. Eisenhower for the presidency. He assisted George C. Craig in becoming national commander of the American Legion, and Craig served as Indiana governor in 1953–57. Sherwood was known as one of Craig's closest advisers, and it was in that regard that he was implicated in a scandal within the state that involved acquiring rights of way for the Indiana Toll Road, a murky development during which several individuals were indicted and convicted in 1958. In 1961 Sherwood served three months in the Indiana state penitentiary.

By this time Elmer Sherwood was no longer young, and like so many Americans of his age he chose to retire to Florida where he purchased three hundred and fifty acres near Lake Sebring, between Sarasota and Vero Beach, named them Sebring Shores, and developed them for sale to homeowners. He was active in Sebring civic affairs and was the inspiration of the International Automobile Hall of Fame and the Sebring Race. He occupied the office of treasurer of the local unit of the Salvation Army. His prominence in Sebring's Rotary Club and nearby clubs persuaded Rotary International to confer on him the prestigious Paul Harris award. He served in the Army Reserve, from which he retired as a brigadier general. He continued his longtime connection with the American Legion.

It was during the Sebring period that the present editor, having begun a book eventually published as *Woodrow Wilson and World War I* (1985), wrote Sherwood and engaged him in a correspondence. We wrote back and forth many times and enjoyed the exchange. Sherwood was a good letter writer. I mentioned the possibility of republishing his diary, with suitable changes, and he was eager to do so, although efforts in that regard did not come to anything. A different effort did come to something. I suggested that he give his diary and papers to the Lilly Library at Indiana University, and he sent them by return mail. We continued to write until, sadly, he died in 1979.

Acknowledgments

IN THE ROSTER OF INDIVIDUALS TO WHOM I AM BEHOLDEN FOR assistance, first are the members of the Sherwood family, and here my great thanks to Joan Sherwood Voyles and Robert Elmer Sherwood, Elmer Sherwood's daughter and son. Robin Sherwood, in the midst of her work in high school, helped in keeping in touch with family members.

E. Bruce Geelhoed of Ball State University generously provided a copy of his unpublished edition of the diaries of Vernon E. Kniptash.

To Saundra Taylor and her staff at the Lilly Library of Indiana University, I owe a debt for bringing out the Sherwood diary and its associated papers, time after time.

The staffs of the National Archives and the U.S. Army Military History Institute, respectively, in College Park, Maryland, and Carlisle, Pennsylvania, provided the necessary background and papers, especially in the persons of, for the Archives, Mitchell Yockelson, and for the Institute its assistant director, Richard J. Sommers.

Many thanks to Thomas A. Mason, vice president of the Indiana Historical Society Press, and to Paula Corpuz, Kathy Breen, Judith McMullen, and George Hanlin of the Press for their readings and most careful advice, all of which I gratefully accepted.

To Lila and Carolyn, I always am grateful. This is the first book to appear without Lila's being able to see it, but she was of so much help.

1 Over There

President Woodrow Wilson disliked preparing for a war that he was unsure the American nation should enter, and even after becoming certain that involvement was necessary, he put off any serious preparation until April 6, 1917, when Congress voted a declaration of war. Wilson permitted the army to draw plans for a draft, rather than relying upon volunteers, but he did little more.

The American military establishment, if one might dignify the peacetime army and navy by such description, was unready for the huge task it faced, which was to raise an army and transport it to France. Months of preparation were necessary before troops could be brought into camp, let alone receive essential equipment. For a while uniforms were lacking. For that matter almost everything was lacking. Near chaos enveloped the War Department in Washington, D.C., just as it had during the Spanish-American War in 1898 and at the outbreak of the Civil War in 1861. It was the American way in war.

In 1917 the army nonetheless managed a massive reorganization. Fort Benjamin Harrison in Indianapolis, a quiet place in peacetime with a semicircle of pleasant officers' houses and nearby barracks where nothing had gone on for years, sprang to life. National Guard units came in and began training. For the draftees it proved necessary to construct huge barrack camps in the North out in country areas with room for maneuvers, and in the South in similarly rural places arose great tent camps—practical, authorities believed, because of the mild weather in winter.

The need to send a few divisions overseas if only as a symbol of eventual American participation in the war persuaded authorities in Washington to create the Forty-second Division, known as the Rainbow Division, a name bestowed upon it by Maj. Douglas MacArthur, who was then a headquarters officer in Washington. Within that division the units, other than its core of four regiments of infantry, each possessing four thousand men, were produced from what MacArthur melodramatically called the rainbow, National Guard troops of twenty-six states and the District of Columbia. Among other units this meant calling up of the First Indiana Field Artillery. Taken into federal service at Fort Harrison, the group became the 150th Field Artillery Regiment. The division's table of organization provided for a three-regiment (each of twelve hundred men, much smaller than infantry regiments) brigade, of which one regiment was to be equipped with heavy guns, and the 150th was chosen to man them.[1]

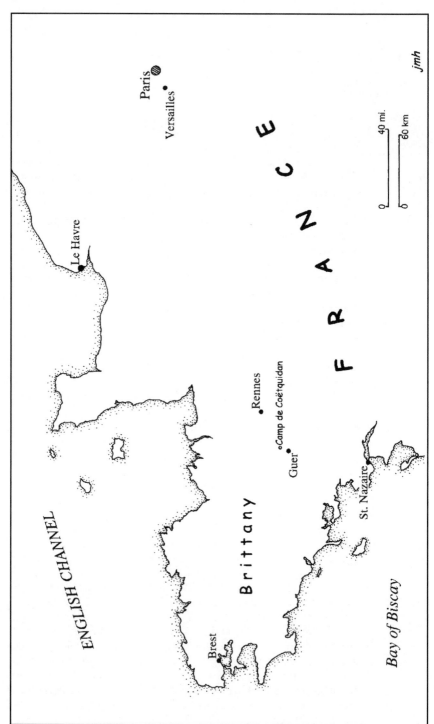

IHS, Bass Photo Company Collection, 61280F

Soldiers firing on rifle range. Many World War I units such as Sherwood's trained at Fort Benjamin Harrison in 1917.

[The source of the narrative that follows is not the diary for this period, until February 1918, which failed to survive, but Sherwood's account in *Rainbow Hoosier*—except entries for the voyage to France that he sent home upon arrival.]

Many of us . . . enlisted in the old First Indiana Regiment of Field Artillery upon the declaration of war, and . . . began our military service when the regiment was assembled at Fort Benjamin Harrison, Indianapolis, August 5, 1917.

Our first craving was for uniforms. How could a fellow feel like a real soldier with only an army hat and a pair of leggins to go with his civilian clothes? Old-timers with extra uniforms, acquired at the [Mexican] border,[2] sold us blouses, shoes, hats and trousers at exorbitant prices, and one fellow was inveigled into buying a boy scout outfit, which he thought was a regulation uniform. Finally, however, our problem was settled when the State of Indiana sold us complete equipment.

In these days when we were told to go on camp police we thought we should carry billies and if assigned to kitchen police we rather expected to be initiated into a lodge. The first row of tents we pitched was as straight as a rail fence. At about this time also our series of inoculations began. A shot in the arm became almost a daily occurrence. Reveille was about the hardest thing for us to become accustomed to. After going to sleep to the strains of some agonized melody, issuing from a neighboring tent, one was not disposed to rise merely at the sound of a bugle. When the Top Cutter yelled "Fall in," a careful observer might detect one fellow minus a leggin, another without his hat, and about ninety per cent of the remainder half asleep. Evenings would see the offenders policing up the camp long after union hours, vowing meanwhile to never let it happen again.[3]

When we joined the First Indiana, we were not only attracted by the spread eagle oratory of patriotic speakers, but the slogan "join the artillery and ride" looked good. However, this proved "the most unkindest cut of all," for on the very first day we began the drill affectionately called squads east and west.

Soon we began to acquire that vague something spoken of in military books as esprit de corp. We were beginning to have a pride in the regiment, which we learned was to be incorporated into the Rainbow (42d) Division, then being organized, and already under orders for early service in France. The regiment's name was to be changed from the First Indiana Field Artillery to the 150th Field Artillery. To be chosen a unit of this crack division was a signal honor, since only the pick of the National Guard troops of the nation were to be selected. The distinction came to the First Indiana because of its fine record as well as the high class of its personnel. In the Spanish-American war a battery went under the name of the Twenty-seventh Volunteer Battery, equipped with 3.2-inch guns. On the border the First Battalion had made one of the best records of the entire army with its three-inch guns.

The officers were all veterans of the organization having enlisted as privates at the beginning of their military service, which varied from two to thirteen years, and in the course of time they had attended various artillery schools of the country. Upon the declaration of war the regiment was expanded into two battalions of three batteries each, light field artillery. Finally, when designated as heavy field artillery of the Rainbow Division, its organization was changed to include three battalions of two batteries each.

At this time our daily schedule left us very few idle hours and our muscles began to toughen with the daily calisthenics, drilling and the manual of arms, and marching. The reward for these days of hard work and practice came September 2d when a great crowd from every part of the State came to Indianapolis to cheer us along the line of march of our farewell parade.

"Even the clouds weep at your departure," said a little girl as the regiment entrained at Fort Harrison for the journey to Long Island, while the rain poured down September seven, however, we were far from being unhappy on that day, for at last we were started on the first stage of our journey to France.

We were fortunate to get Pullmans for the journey and after our strenuous month of drilling we could appreciate our comforts. Many were the innocent victims who received their first lessons in the old army game as the train sped through the Lehigh Valley and past the beautiful Lake Seneca.[4]

IHS, Bass Photo Company Collection, 61282F

Gov. and Mrs. James P. Goodrich meeting with troops at Fort Benjamin Harrison, Indianapolis, 1917. Forces training to go overseas generated a great deal of enthusiasm from local dignitaries and the general population.

We arrived at Camp Mills, Long Island, on the evening of the ninth, where we took our places in the Rainbow's tented city. The wind-swept and dusty plain upon which our camp was situated was not an ideal location, but we made our battery streets attractive by covering them with gravel.

Two days in the week we were given time off, and we took advantage of such days by going on pass to the nearby towns of Hempstead and Garden City, or to New York.[5] The wonders of the big city attracted the greater majority, and natives of such Hoosier cities as Tulip and Columbia City became more familiar with Coney, Sherry's and the Winter Garden than the staid New Yorkers themselves.[6] Others preferred to mingle in the fashionable society of the Island, attending the functions of the dowagers, who simply had to help win the war some way. Naturally, we shone with brilliancy at these affairs, aided by our newly acquired army manners and our heavy army shoes which so greatly facilitated our dancing upon the slippery hardwood floors.

Two entertainments, greatly enjoyed by all of us, were those given by the 151st F.A. and the 149th F.A. In the division, besides special and auxiliary units, there were two brigades of infantry and one brigade of artillery. The brigade of artillery was the 67th, consisting of the 149th and 151st

IHS, Bass Photo Company Collection, 61285F

Soldiers resting. Although Sherwood found the constant drilling exhausting, he felt that it was necessary in preparing the troops for combat in France.

regiments of 75s, light field artillery, and the 150th and 155th millimeter howitzers, light-heavy field artillery. To promote a feeling of comradeship among the men of the brigade, each regiment was to give an entertainment for the other two. We left Camp Mills for France before we could give our entertainments, but those of the Illinois and Minnesota outfits were great successes. They consisted of feasting, singing, rendering college yells, and in attending the vaudeville shows, which featured on the program, pugilists, black-faced artists, jazz bands and Oriental dancers.

In speaking of our diversions I do not wish to convey the idea that our path was strewn with roses, for the greater part of our time was spent in hard work. Our daily schedule called for eight hours of drill and our drill grounds were rough and broken, which made the drilling all the more exhausting. In fact, even the long hikes over the dusty Long Island roads came as a relief, though our dirty trips necessitated bathing under the ice-cold showers. The baths were protected from the chilly ocean breezes by thin canvas walls.

Though the drills were hard we realized their benefits when the entire division was reviewed by the Secretary of War [Newton D. Baker]. If we made good that day we knew that we would soon be sent "across," so every man was on his mettle. The Rainbow Division was the first tactical division assembled and reviewed in the United States after the declaration of war. The parade of the twenty-eight thousand men at Garden City made a great impression. The New York newspapers were overflowing with the division's praises and cited it as a proof of Uncle Sam's prowess and as a warning to the Kaiser.

Secretary Baker was impressed by the review, and though our numbers were not great in terms of European armies, our ranks contained more soldiers than were actually engaged in fighting in the Spanish-American war for the United States. It had been Mr. Baker's contention that a crack division could be formed from the pick of National Guard regiments and he found his dream on this day realized when the Rainbows, assembled from twenty-six states, passed in review before him.[7]

[The following is the shipboard diary published in the *Linton Citizen* after Sherwood's arrival in France].[8]

OCT. 18 We arose at three o'clock this morning and in two hours were marching with full pack and rifle to the station where we entrained for the river docks where ferry boats carried us up the river, to the piers, where the big ocean liners flying the U.S. flag were waiting to carry us to foreign soil.

All day long thousands of Sammies [soldiers] who were to make the voyage were arriving and going up the gangplank in single file. Each of us was given a slip of paper on which was printed the deck compartment and bunk each was to occupy and where we were to eat and wash.

Everything has to be arranged as efficiently as possible so that the ships can be filled to capacity. You would be surprised at the great number of troops which this vessel, the length of which is almost two Linton blocks, can carry.

We left at night pulled by six tugs. I stayed on deck until call to quarters was blown, when I went below to my bunk on the second deck.

OCT. 19 I arose at five-thirty and after a bath was ready for breakfast. Our mess is very good, consisting of soup, vegetables, meat, bread, butter, coffee, and the best bread and butter I ever ate. When I came on deck this morning I was greeted with my first view of the ocean with no land in view. I had planned all my life to make a voyage across the sea, but I little thought it would be under the conditions existing now. The fact is that very few people have been privileged to travel as we are doing now. We are a part of a great fleet. Our transports, of which we are the flagship, are guarded by ships of the U.S. Navy. Tonight I am sitting on the top deck after looking out on the mighty ocean upon which our big ship is but a speck.

I am reminded of Byron's poem of the ocean, where he describes the strength of the ocean compared with man. "Roll on, thou dark and deep blue Ocean—roll! Ten thousand fleets sweep over thee in vain." Here on the top of the ship I lie between my blankets in silence. All have gone to their bunks except some like myself who prefer to lie on deck. What an opportunity for one to think. He cannot help it. The great waves dash against the sides of the ship but one does not notice them for their monotony. I can realize now why so many boys leave their homes to seek adventure on the high seas, and why so many old tars would not quit the sailor's life for any money.

The only light is furnished by the moon and stars. I wish I knew more about them. I see the big dipper and Venus, and the North Star, but I know almost nothing of them. Scientists know comparatively little about them, I suppose, but I can realize why they are so interesting, that men never tire of studying them and war cannot change them in the least.

OCT. 20 We have encountered a rough sea today and as a result almost everyone is seasick. The rails are lined with sick, cold troops who have no further use for their dinners. Some of the scenes are almost indescribable, but through it all I have managed to keep well and eat heartily.

I think there is good reason to use Christian Science for I know I could be sick if I wanted to be.[9]

Our day included two hours of physical drill at 9 a.m. [The remainder of the day's work was cut out by the censor.]

OCT. 21 This being Sunday we had chicken for dinner. Our meals have been good all the way and though we are inactive and not really hungry we manage to eat as much as usual. The seasickness has passed from most of the boys and comparatively few hang over the rails to feed the fish. Tonight I lay out on deck for several hours, looking at the sea and sky. It never gets tiresome. I saw a phenomenon of which I had never heard. There is absolutely no light visible from the boat and yet in the wake of the vessel, where the water is churned into a milky whiteness, it sparkles and . . . [illegible] casting out so much light that one can almost read by it. The sailors told me it was phosphorus.

OCT. 22 I saw several sea gulls today and was inclined to think we were nearing land but I understand they go hundreds of miles from land. Henry Sisk from Linton is in the same battery as I and is on the same boat as are Claude Moulden, Flemming and

Arthur Lynch also of Linton. Sisk bunks under me and I see the other boys every day.

In the battery are two full-blooded Indians, Kane and Island, fine fellows. I think how wonderful the contrast is today from the time when Columbus in his little sailboats first came to America, which was peopled solely by the Indians. Today some of these Indians are going to the Old World in a great steamboat. I never realized how brave such men as Columbus and his followers were until now. At any time I can look back and see one of the big liners in our fleet rock on the big waves. The fellows on this boat are very anxious to see land because of sickness, monotony, etc. Think of Columbus and his men; they didn't know where they were going, and some thought they would fall off the edge of the earth, and their hopes of seeing land before their food gave out were small, and yet they persisted.

OCT.
23

[Much of this entry was cut out by the censor.] When a gun is shot the sound is terrific. The crew stuff their ears with cotton and the rest of us stand on our toes with our mouths open to prevent the eardrums breaking; however, the seeing of these guns in action made me desire to get to work on ours.

OCT.
24

All morning I have been carrying one-hundred-pound sacks of flour from the hatch to the top deck up steep stairs, but I have no kick coming, because it is the first work I have done on the ship and I stood it all night and we have most of our time to rest anyway. [More cut by the censor. The diary of the voyage ends here, with return to the narrative in *Rainbow Hoosier*.]

The wonders of the ocean commanded our interest for a time; but on the third day out we encountered a rough sea and about ninety per cent of our number were filled with the commendable desire to feed the fish. "Two-bits he comes," became an expression not only of the crap game but of the deck. However, those who were not affected at the start managed to endure the indescribable scenes and kept up a hearty appetite. . . .

At all times of the day we were required to wear our life preservers and at night we used them as pillows. There were so many men aboard that it required an entire day to feed the three meals. Each day the monotony of walking this never-ending mess line was varied by one hour of physical exercise and one hour of submarine drill.

By this time we refused to be worried about our chances of dodging submarines. In fact, only once was a sub sighted and it turned tail when one of our destroyers started after it. Nevertheless we learned our proper places on the decks and when the alarm sounded we lost no time in getting there.[10]

For protection we had not only convoy of two destroyers and a cruiser, "Seattle," but our own transports were equipped with naval guns, manned by sailors. On the ninth day of the voyage these tars demonstrated their prowess at target practice. The targets, representing submarine periscopes, were drawn behind each vessel of the fleet and each gun of each vessel took its turn at firing, the ranges varying from a half-mile to two miles. All shots were close and many hits were made. A peculiar feature of firing on the water is that after a shell strikes the water and it disappears it will again emerge into the air and travel a mile or so farther, when it will again strike the sea with a splash resembling a water spout. The distance of this rico-chet depends upon the angle of fire, the sailors say. The convoys ran down tramp steamers and searched all vessels which came within sight. Half-way out the steamer Grant, which carried the 167th (Alabama) Infantry of our division and incidentally contained the horses of our regiment, turned back as its boilers went bad.[11]

The longer we were at sea the more we came to admire Columbus for sticking it out on his journey in a sailboat when the odds were against him. The monotony began to wear on us and the rolling of the ship became unpleasant. At any time one could look back over the fleet and see the giant steel vessels rocking in the rough sea, while life must have been mis-erable on the destroyers, which were tossed about like chips and at times could not be seen beneath the waves.

On the 28th word was received that a U-boat was approaching the fleet.[12] This occasioned some concern among the few higher officers, who had received the news, because the new convoy, which was scheduled to meet us on this day, had not yet arrived. We were following the usual zigzag course but at the news changed direction. Next day the convoy of eight additional destroyers, which were camouflaged so as to be almost indis-cernable at a distance, joined us. As the fleet neared Belle Isle it was sig-nalled to follow a submarine chaser, which guided our ships another course to avoid the submarines which were lying in wait in the path which we were to have taken.[13]

When we went on deck the morning of the thirtieth, land was in view. Our life preservers, affectionately called sinkers, were now discarded, to our great relief. The following night, Halloween, we reached the port of St. Nazaire as the band played "Good-bye Broadway, Hello France."

During our four days of inaction aboard ship in the port, venders of chocolate and fruits acted as our medium with the shore. These poor peo-ple came out to us in their little boats, which were propelled by a single oar at the stern and operated by a person standing. We tied out [our] hats to long ropes, dropped in some coin and lowered them down the side of the ship, where they were grasped by the wooden-shoed Frogs, who removed the money and replaced it with their wares.[14] One had to be careful in bringing it back up that it didn't tip and spill the contents and also had to avoid the greedy hands sticking out of the portholes below.

On the morning of November fifth, our entire brigade disembarked and marched to camp on the outskirts of the town. It was a great and glorious feeling to set foot on terra firma again and this time it was the soil of France; henceforth our address was covered by the general term of "Somewhere in France." Our camp was the first of the so-called rest variety, many of which we were destined to occupy and to find that the only rest we were supposed to get was in the darkest night. Hikes, drills and engineering details were our forms of diversions.

St. Nazaire is a typical seaport town and we will remember it as the place where we were first introduced to the French language and vin rouge. Soon we acquired a few words of French and then expected to be understood by the shopkeepers. If they did not "Compree" we would become quite riled and were apt to claim that the Frogs simply refused to try to understand. Oftentimes one of them would start rattling off a string of French and the Yank would enter the argument with good old "United States" and an endurance contest would result.

Some of the boys tried to get away with stage French, such as "Ze genteelman wishees some of zee food.". . .

In the small hours of November eighteenth we hiked to the station and boarded the funny little compartment coaches of a French railroad. After a long day's ride we arrived at Guer, where we detrained and began our hike to the training camp. When we reached our barracks that night our weary spirits were revived by receiving the first mail since leaving the States.

[Sherwood's brigade had entrained for the French artillery reservation known as Camp Coëtquidan, which artillerists had used since the time of Napoleon. While at the camp, the regiments received their guns and learned how to fire them.]

Camp Coëtquidan is one of the oldest artillery schools in France and is situated in the ancient province of Brittany. The buildings in the camp consisted of the old French barracks which had been used as prison camps and three large concrete buildings. The concrete buildings came to be used as a hospital by our brigade and the wooden barracks were destined to be our home for fourteen weeks. They were heated or were supposed to be heated by small stoves and our bunks were made on platforms which ran the length of the buildings on both sides. The entire camp had been deloused by the men of the second battalion which outfit had preceded the rest of the regiment a week for that purpose. Notwithstanding their effort, some of the men acquired these pests here for the first time.

The surrounding country is very attractive with its monotony broken by wooded and cultivated hills. The natives are not progressive, however, and live in houses built in past ages. They are, in fact, poorer than the inhabitants of any other district of France, using the methods of industry and agriculture long ago discarded in America. During our stay here we were allowed a few passes to Rennes, the ancient capital of Brittany. It is a more progressive city, and contains architecture of the modern age as well as of the past. Its main industry at this time was the making of munitions. Women ran the street cars and had taken the place of men in all sorts of industries. We came in contact with soldiers of almost all Allies, especially the Russians, whose hospitals were here. And let me say here that these men of the Russian legion who had been wounded on the French front were among the finest soldiers I ever saw. If the Russians had been properly directed and equipped they would have proved equal to the Germans on the Eastern front.

Along the road past Coëtquidan many peddlers and tradesmen established shops, so that soon the route began to resemble a country fair, where we could buy everything from wine to souvenirs. Even Charles Chaplin made his appearance regularly at the cinema.

For four or five francs we could buy a meal consisting first of soup, a broth containing bits of bread. This was brought in a bowl from which one helped himself. The next course was a meat, steak, or perhaps a fish; if a fish, the head and tail was included. If one was lucky he might get chicken, though the chances were that he would have to wait until the hostess went out and caught it. Next came French fried potatoes, followed by a salad and often cheese and an apple. Often snails were served as a side dish. Pins were furnished as weapons with which to extract the meat from the tiny shells. A knife was always given with a loaf of bread, so that the diner might cut it himself. This delicate operation is executed by holding the loaf in the arms and cutting the slice at one stroke. Coffee was served if asked for. In reality it consisted of cognac, milk and a small proportion of coffee. A bottle of wine was, of course, always served at four or five francs additional cost. About all the French use water for is to wash clothes in. If one asked for it the waitress might have to make a special visit to the town pump.

From the first day our schedule at camp was strenuous, for we had only a limited time in which to learn how to man the new French six-inch howitzers, with which we were equipped. The 149th and 151st were, of course, receiving their instruction in the use of the French 75s at the same time. During our training period, Brigadier-General C. P. Summerall, who had been commander of the 67th Brigade since its organization, was promoted in rank to Major-General, and was given command of the First Division. Later he was made commander of the 5th Corps and he commanded it in the Meuse-Argonne offensive when we served in that unit.

Brigadier-General [Charles H.] McKinstry succeeded him in command of our brigade and served in that capacity through the Lorraine Campaign. When in Champagne, on July thirteenth, he was succeeded by Brigadier-General George C. Gatley, who held the command until the armistice was signed.

Our divisional commanders were also frequently changed. Major-General [William A.] Mann, who was placed in command of the division at its organization, returned to the States while we were in training at Coëtquidan. Upon his return to America he made the statement that the

67th Brigade, consisting of the 149th (Illinois) and 151st (Minnesota) Regiments of light field artillery and the 150th (Indiana) Regiment of light-heavy field artillery, was the best brigade of artillery in France, regardless of the classifications, Regular Army, National Guard and National Army.[15]

Major-General Charles T. Menoher now became our commander and he led the division through the war, receiving the highest credit from his superiors and being presented with the highest medals of honor bestowed by the American army and the Allies. When he was promoted to a higher position, Major-General [Charles D.] Rhodes, Brigadier-General Douglas MacArthur, and Major-General C. F. A. [C. A. F.] Flagler succeeded to the command in turn.

Colonel Robert H. Tyndall, of Indianapolis, commanded the regiment from its organization to the day it was mustered out. At Camp Mills, the guard who was walking post before the Colonel's tent, was confronted by a man past middle age, who wanted to know if this was where Robert Tyndall was bunking. When he received an affirmative answer he entered the tent. He emerged an hour later wearing a broad smile and he addressed the guard, "Say, Buddy, he knew me the first thing. You see we were bunkies together back in '98 in Puerto Rico, and, believe me, he didn't have a big tent like this one. No siree, he was a plain old buck private like yourself," and he went on his way chuckling and murmering, "Same old Robert." The buck started and thought, "Gee whiz, a buck; wonder if he kept his puts shined up then like he does now."[16]

That illustrated the military career of the Colonel "Bob," for he had kept in the military life since he had joined Battery A, 1st Indiana Field Artillery, in the Spanish-American War days. He held every rank up to major, in which capacity he served on the Mexican border, and in the natural course of events he became commander of Indiana's Rainbow Regiment when the United States declared war on Germany.

Our instructors were French officers and sergeants, who had been in the fighting from the start of the war. Several enlisted men of the First Division were also detailed to teach us what they had learned of the art in the quiet sectors which they had occupied.

Our course was enlarged when the horse boats arrived and the famous command "stand to heel" became an obsession. However, we had received our hardest knocks in horseback riding at Fort Harrison and we knew we could stick on any of the wild ones here. We began to be divided into special classes, for instance, the cannoneers learned the operation of the pieces, the drivers learned to harness their teams and to maneuver the pieces into different positions, while signal men specialized in telephone and wireless.

Soon after Thanksgiving when our corned willie menu was displaced by a real, old-fashioned turkey dinner, we began firing our big guns on the range.[17] This introduction to the roaring guns was not so pleasant as one

IHS, Robert H. Tyndall Collection, C8069

Col. Robert H. Tyndall. Tyndall was a well-respected and popular officer who began his military career in the Spanish-American War.

IHS, Bass Photo Company Collection, 61286F

Dining hall. Food, according to Sherwood, was a soldier's obsession.

would suppose, for the intonation of a six-inch gun is terrific, and the use of cotton in the ears will not prevent one from hearing it, in fact, the tingle would be in our ears after a night's sleep. Naturally, we became accustomed to the noise and felt just as natural while they were roaring as when they were silent.

Later we were instructed in the use of gas masks and as a part of the course passed through a chamber filled with the real article. Trench digging and dug-out construction were entered into, and every man was taught the use of the rifle or pistol in target practice.

Our first Christmas on foreign soil was the banner holiday of the year, of course, and carloads of boxes from home came to our regiment alone. Besides boxes of good things from the folks, each man received a box of candy from the Rainbow Cheer Association of Indiana. Every man had more knitted goods of various sizes than he could use for there was a special craze for knitting at the time in the States. Our dinner was fine, with turkey and sweet stuffs galore; of course, this was not the usual fare; ordinarily we had light stew or heavy stew, or soup, all known by the edifying name of slum-gullion. We were assured that the best food went to the trenches, and, later, when we reached the trenches, we found that somebody had circulated a false rumor, for army grub is the same everywhere.

Speaking of food, I must say that chow is a soldier's obsession; if he can not get what he wants he can at least talk about it and dream about it. At any time of the night a certain fellow of our outfit might be expected to break into a discourse upon food, perhaps describing in detail the hot biscuits his mother used to make, and how he had always put gobs of golden butter in between, or he might describe in detail pies of every known species and variety. Of course a shower of footwear would cause him to desist, but always he would add, "Oh! them wuz the days."

On the morning of February twenty-first we were awakened at three o'clock and we all knew that it was moving day. It was raining, but that couldn't dampen our enthusiasm. We were full of "pep" and worked like blazes to get everything out of camp and on to the trains at the Guer station. We left training camp with the best record which had been made there, surprising alike ourselves and our instructors. Credit was due the officers for their initiative and resourcefulness as well as to the men for their enthusiasm, despite knee-deep mud and their adaptability to all branches of artillery work.

2 | Lunéville Sector
(FEBRUARY–MARCH 1918)

Detached from the Forty-second Division to train at the French artillery camp, the Sixty-seventh Field Artillery Brigade that included the 150th Field Artillery Regiment rejoined the division in a sector in Alsace that extended from the western slope of the Vosges Mountains to the northeast for thirty-five kilometers, twenty-two miles, a part of the western front that extended from the Channel to Switzerland. Three French divisions occupied the Lunéville sector and supervised the training of the American division. At the end of training the Forty-second assembled near the town of Gerbéviller and moved to another sector.

The Vosges rest camp, as the men later described it, gave the division its first opportunity to deploy as a unit. Camp Mills had been little more than a place for transit.

Lunéville in the Vosges also offered a chance to fire a few shots at the Germans, which the men seized, against the advice of their instructors who told them, "If you fire against the Bosches they will fire against you." German troops in the hitherto quiet sector added the special retaliation of poison gas, dousing the Americans with this real-life portion of war on the western front. The Americans used their masks, not easy to work in or sleep with, and considered the exercise a necessary learning experience.

Meanwhile the division made the acquaintance of local villagers, supplementing army cooking with eggs purchased from villagers. Otherwise the most popular dietary supplement was liquid, the ever-present vin rouge, together with local vintages, usually cognac.

FEB.
21

This is the beginning of a new book but I can plainly see that it isn't going to contain as much writing as my diary of 1917, because at the front no doubt time will be very limited.[1]

Left camp this morning at 7:00 and loaded at Guer. The whole bunch worked like blazes and we made a record for entraining. It seemed an immense train when we were set to go with the guns, wagons, caissons, and supplies on flat cars followed by horse cars and then by the box cars occupied by us. 40 x 8[2]

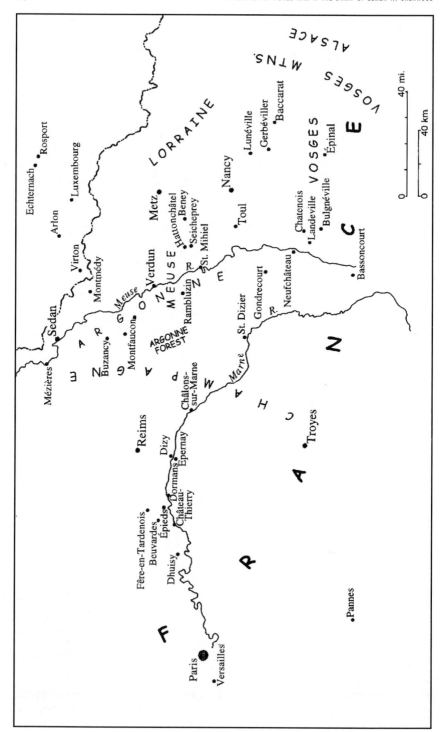

FEB.
22

Even the hay in the car doesn't make sleeping easy but we got thru the night and welcomed morning. Its my birthday and of course the guys had to paddle me 22 times. Passed Versailles today and saw Eiffel Tower in the distance but didn't stop.

FEB.
23

We rose at 3:30 a.m. and rolled our packs because the lieut. said we would probably detrain within an hour but it proved to be a false alarm and we rode until 5:30 p.m.

This is Lorrain[e] and of course was in German hands in 1914 at the beginning of the war. Everybody waves at us just as the people did while we were journeying from Indianapolis to New York.

We reached our destination in the evening at 4:30 [?] and unloaded at 7:00 mess was ready and we filed past the kitchen wagon for beans. It sure was a welcome meal.

Then we hitched up the horses to caissons, guns and wagons and loaded trucks and began the journey to our billets. I rode a truck and was surprised at the speed it made in the pitch dark (no lights allowed) but the roads were fine and it was only an hour until we reached the town where we were to stop for a couple of days. It was after midnight when we had finished tying up the horses and unloading the wagons and we were mighty glad when we were conducted to our respective hay lofts for the night.[3]

FEB.
24

Got up at 9:30 because we had no reville. It is a vacation in itself to be able to sleep late. I heard a rooster crow this morning when I woke up and thinking it was one of the fellows trying to act funny as they often do, I picked up a shoe ready to throw at him when I came out of my slumbers more I realized that it really was a rooster.

Nitz, Brown and I went to a neighboring town this morning in search of milk and eggs. Some men, women, and children are again living in the slightly damaged houses amidst the ruins. Many Africans are billeted here as well as a few French and they all seem to get along fine.[4]

We bought some eggs and at one house where we had a chat with a group of peasants three girls, two women, and two men they got a good deal of enjoyment out of our accent when we spoke French but we made them understand viz I wanted some milk which is de lait but they couldn't get me so I drew a picture of a cow on an egg putting six tits on the udder. The women said no no and I didn't understand for a good while what they were talking about when they said cat (4). I wasn't trying to make a technical drawing but I had to change it.

The inhabitants of this locality are very sensible as well as congenial. I bought eggs of a woman and then asked if she would sell a pouli (chicken) and she said, no poulies no erf (eggs). They do not want to sell the chickens for any price. When I left the house I said merci and the little child corrected me saying merci madam.

FEB. 25

Revellie at 6:15 and after breakfasting everybody shaved and washed in the town troughs gee but it was a grand and glorious feeling to be clean again. We hiked in the morning also and passed many French regiments on the march to the front. They are fine looking soldiers and I believe will make good fighting partners; but they don't sing and laugh as they go marching by the reason being that they have been doing this for 4 years.

We get all the milk we can drink and the eggs we can eat here and believe me we take full advantage of it. The hay in the loft makes, by far, the best bunks we have had since leaving America.

The town in which we live was taken from the Germans by the French after a 17 days battle and the town surely is a wreck. Among the ruins one can pick up parts of shells etc, but among the mass of ruins are a few houses which were slightly damaged and have since been repaired and in these the inhabitants, who are left, live. These houses are really barns with living rooms built in one part and with stables adjacent the upper story is the hay loft and here we lived.

All inhabitants as well as French soldiers are very kind, polite and friendly and are of a much better sort than those with whom we came in contact in Brittany.

FEB. 26

Lieut. Gasper and nine men of the detail mounted started from the town at 7 a.m. It felt fine to be in the saddle again and I had one of the best mounts in the battery. At one place I was sent back to deliver an order to an officer of A Battery which was following us and my horse sure made time. He is the fastest horse I ever rode and I let him out. After I delivered the message I rejoined the detail.

At noon we reached the wood where battery B was to have its wagon line. We heard the old cannons roar all the time but it didn't even make us chilley rather I was anxious to go on up; But after lunching we took our axes and began downing trees and cutting logs preparing for the arrival of the battery. We made picket lines and cut brush for the boys to sleep on. Yes we did the real pioneer stunt. It was my first experience at chopping trees but I enjoyed it in spite of the fatigue.

We had our first glimpse of an enemy aeroplane. It had come over our lines and our anti-aircraft batteries turned loose on it. Shells were exploding all around the Boche—the smoke from them is suspended in the air for about a half a minute and one can trace the progress of the machine by them.

The battery arrived at dusk and the guns went into their positions while all other wagons came to the wagon line which we had prepared. It was tough work for the horses to pull their loads up the muddy hill but all of us helped by pulling with a rope and by 1 a.m. everything was set and the boys began rolling into blankets on the ground. Ingram and I pitched our little pup tent and laid our blankets underneath and crawled in for a fine night's rest. I remembered of grandpa telling me how he used to pile up some brush on the wet ground and roll into his blankets under the starry sky when he was with [Gen. William T.] Sherman.

FEB.
27

It rained last night but the pup kept us dry and we had a fine sleep. The detail has started running the telephone lines now the first one from wagon line to gun positions will be completed today. Our rations are poor now consisting almost exclusively of coffee, bacon and hard tack.

The night firing is quite a sight the flash of guns lights up the sky and star shells and rockets over no man's land look like a big 4th of July celebration.

FEB.
28

We stood muster and signed the pay roll today. Then helped French soldiers in construction of new barracks which we will occupy.

Afternoon Fisher and I ran a line to battalion. In wading thru the water covered fields we both went into water over our boots and worked the rest of the day with our feet soaking wet. (If mother could only see me now?) But we got the line thru and had communications by night fall. Its tough to work hard all day and have little of nothing to eat.

National Archives

Battery D, 150th Field Artillery (formerly First Indiana Field Artillery), camouflaging and building dugouts, Reherrey, France, March 1918. Dugouts and camouflaging were necessary to conceal the positions of troops and artillery from enemy airplanes.

MAR.
1

Detail started work on telephone dug out today; and it is no soft job digging in this mud. We get up at 4:00 and work until 6 p.m. Not much romance to that? but we all know that it has to be done and we're digging for our own protection. We drop into dead slumber when we hit our bunks.

MAR.
2

Another day of real toil is passed and when it is over we are too tired to read or write or wash (even if we had water).

MAR.
3

We begin to see what we have accomplished now dugouts, ammunition pits and gun pits are getting to look like something. Of course we have to camafladg as we go along, thereby concealing ourselves from enemy areoplanes. We have to wear our gas masks at all times just as we wore life preservers on the boat; but, they may come in handy, tho they are an awful nuisance while we are working.[5]

MAR.
4

I operated phone at Ashlon[6] today and installed a phone in officers quarters with the help of Schwartz. Since I didn't do manual labor today I had nerve enough to walk down to Montiniere (two miles toward the first lines) to see if I could get something to eat and sure enuff there was a YMCA canteen there.

There was unusual artillery activity on the front tonight and Lavoie, who was with me became skeptical as to the advisability of go on for he said tho he wanted food he preferred his life; but I urged him on and we got there. The Y.M.C.A. sect said he didn't like the language the Huns were using but he was sticking to his post, tho shells were landing in his back yard.[7] The fire works over no man's land was pretty and I resolved to go down to see the doughboys as soon as I could get off duty at the battery.

MAR.
5

The best news of the day is that tonight we get a new issue of food. We dug as usual today. The second section has completed its dug out and will sleep there from now on.

I am on guard tonight at 11 p.m. About twenty men from the horse detail arrived and I had to find places for them to sleep, then put up the six horses which they had brought.

MAR.
6

As we were eating mess this noon when three big sedans cars drove up the road and stopped back of our gun position. The door of the first car was opened and out stepped General [John J.] Pershing. He is not a disappointment to the hero worshipper but is every inch a soldier and he is a six footer at that. He has a good looking intelligent face and has the finest carrige.

He came up to the mess line and asked the buck who was getting his kit filled how he liked the army life and if he was getting plenty to eat. He then inspected our gun positions and was well satisfied. When he drove away he left one proud fellow at least, the lucky dog with whom he talked.

MAR. 7

We fired our first shot today. A battery did likewise and probably the other batteries of the regiment did also.

I was on the battery end of the phone and received all the data from the observatory and gave it to the guns.

MAR. 8

Operated switchboard all day with Hughes and Fisher stayed with me thruout the night. We wrote letters until late.

MAR. 9

Usual day of digging. If this was what we would always have to do I should say that the war is an awful bore. We sure are digging ourselves in, and one can plainly see why it takes so long to fight this kind of a war.

MAR. 10

Our digging day was varied by running a telephone line from our dug out to the machine gun emplacement on the crest of the hill.

MAR. 11

Spent the day in camafladging work at the guns. At 7 p.m. I started out to our forward gun position with a guard detail. All our caissons went up loaded with ammunition which we had to guard.

It was dark when we got up there but we managed to find an old gun pit where we could spread our blankets and be somewhat shielded from the wind. There was no roof of course so we could lie on our backs and see the fourth of July celebration out on no man's land.

Well, here we were a little detail of three men and myself. It was cold and of course our feet were wet. I shivered the night thru on account of the cold and not because I minded the noise of the shells because we couldn't see them in the night any way, I mean exclusive of star shells and rockets.

MAR.
12
Toward morning the Deutsch gave a battery a quarter of a mile from us a terrific bombardment. Then some came toward us. In fact they lit all about us. We would duck when we heard the old zzz of the shell and when she lit and bursted we would find that it was away off.

At dawn they sent over some gas and before we knew what it was I felt my nose burn and I repeatedly sneezed the other fellows had the same symptoms; but no one was hurt because the gas was not heavy where we were.

In the morning the town to our left is getting a bunch of Hun shells. Sherer and I went over the fields in front of our pit and saw several shell holes made during the night.

In the afternoon the Germans shelled an old battery position a quarter of a mile directly in front of us. It was funny to see the shells come over and to think of the thousands of dollars they were wasting.

At nightfall our caissons came again loaded with shells and after they were unloaded we climbed on and were taken back to eschelon while another guard detail stayed this night.

When we get enough shells up the battery will pull up and whale away at the Huns.

MAR.
13
Sgt. Fultz, another Elk, who is in the medical corps and myself rode to a neighboring town, where F battery is located to get our teeth fixed. The dentist was gone so we returned.

In the afternoon two Hun planes flew back of our lines, attacking an observation baloon in our rear. Just as one machine gun of one of the planes opened fire on the baloon one of the shells from our anti-aircraft batteries brought the machine down. The other one turned tail and flew but before he reached his own lines he also was hit but managed to light within his own lines.

MAR.
14
At gun position all day as usual. We are going farther front tomorrow.

MAR.
15
During the night our guns were put in position a mile from German lines and in the morning we began firing.

I was on the phone at battery and received the data from the Radio, who got it from the aviator who was observing our fire.

We were laid on a German 77 battery and the aviator reported in the evening that we had completely destroyed the battery. Our first big scalp.

National Archives

Battery C, 150th Field Artillery (formerly First Indiana Field Artillery), firing near Vailly, France, March 15, 1918.

MAR.

16

Continued pouring lead into the Huns thru out the day and in evening drew our guns back to our regular position. As we were pulling out the Germans were getting our range and some shells came close; but too late Fritz.

MAR.

17

The Huns gave us our first casualties today. While our fellows were constructing a dug out a HE shell came over and exploded in the dug out.[8] Kenny Hughes, Glass, Yates and Fabian were wounded and are in the hospital now. Yate[s]'s leg was blown off and I do not know how badly the others were injured. Just yesterday Kenny and I were joking about wounded cheverons.

MAR.

18

A detail of nine men were assigned single mounts today and henceforth they will be ours to use and take care of. I got "Rabbits," only seven hands high but a 'goer' and the prettiest horse in the outfit.

MAR. 19

My title is range finder and if we drive Fritz out of the trenches and fight him in the open I will have a lot of duties being always in the van.

"Rabbits" will follow me around and has already made friends with me.

MAR. 20

Today we completed the telephone dug out and believe me we are glad because it has been the toughest job any of us ever had, and tho we know it is necessary it isn't much fun to fight with a pick and shovel?

We will install our switchboard and lines in the hole now and make arrangements for sleeping quarters in it.

It has, however been a great experience to start at the beginning and make a battery position and doing it all the while in a secret manner not to make the Huns suspicious. From now on we are cave dwellers.

MAR. 21

Spent morning in camouflaging at gun position. It is one of the essentials of modern warfare yet it isn't peculiar to this war even Shakespere told about how the old timers used boughs to conceal their armies and how the advancing army resembled a moving forest was it in Macbeth?

We are moving back of the line to a rest camp presumably, so we have all our material packed and ready to leave in the morning. We have emptied our bed ticks and are sleeping on the boards tonight.

We have been through one baptism of fire—a sort of test of courage. There were no nervous Nellies—mental crackups. A contributing factor of our wonderful es prit de corps of the Rainbow is that we are volunteers. We wanted to fight for our country. This Loraine front was more or less static so we look forward to more action and fighting as Pershing wants to attack out of the trenches.

MAR. 22

At 2 a.m. battery arose and two hours later we were on the way to rest camp.

Fritz must have had a suspicion of our leaving (possibly from our bonfire) for he gave us a royal send off, shelling all about the wood. Everybody was glad to get out on the open road and to go ahead.

We arrived at the town where we were to [be] billeted temporarily at 10:30, so we put up our picket line and made ourselves "to home" in the lofts of the town.

Tho this town was at one time occupied by the Germans it is not such a pile of ruins as many in this zone.

MAR.	As usual Ichabod is my bunkie. He has a very bad case of boils
23	which requires the attention of both of us. With the usual stables

As usual Ichabod is my bunkie. He has a very bad case of boils which requires the attention of both of us. With the usual stables we manage to get time for a little loafing and some football. We are feasting on eggs and milk which we buy from the natives.

MAR. 24 This is palm Sunday and of course the people of the town are wearing their finest and I was surprised at the difference it made in the people. Even the girls looked pretty. Our band has arrived and gave a concert today and of course the town square was crowded with soldiers and civilians. The latter were much amused by the dancing in the street by some of the Sammies.

MAR. 25 Our plans have been changed and we are to stay here a week and then go back to the front. There is snow about now that the regiment is to be motorized.[9]

MAR. 26 We have bareback riding every day. Today I was acting "cute" and riding Rabbits backward and he bucked me off. On our rides we go thru thickets woods and other difficult places, at the same time we get to see much of the surrounding country. We are in a beautiful locality of rolling hills and in the distance the Vosges loom up.

The people of the village are very agreeable and when I go to buy milk at one of the houses I always stay and visit awhile. They have a cute little boy who likes to fight.

MAR. 27 The mounted detail rides to certain positions every day and figures out dope as in actual action. Barbar and Gasper always accompany us.

The town crier made his rounds today. He rolled his drum, said a few words rolled it again and then read a proclamation to the people who had gathered about.

The people of this locality spade up their fields. It is funny to watch them women, boys and old men they sure do spade up a field in quick time. The loss of young men has made it necessary for old people to work and it is a pitiful sight to see decrepit old men and women working.

The old woman in whose loft we live crochets handkerchiefs which she sells at Baccarat. She talks to me a great deal while she sits out in front of her home. She told about the cruelty of the Boche when they occupied the town and she hasn't gotten over the horror of it yet.

MAR.
28

Every day I go over to the wireless station to get news of the new Hun drive. It is like listening to election returns; each side makes great claims and the Boche is proclaiming it the last battle of the war; but he has been stopped and now watch us crack him.

We received mail today—sure is a pleasure to hear from home—one letter contained pictures of Dad and Mom, which I had been looking for a long time.

3 | Baccarat

On March 21, when the Forty-second Division began to move into the Baccarat sector, where it would remain for several months, the German army opened the first of five huge offensives against the Allies. Each offensive became less threatening, until they gradually petered out. During the last of the offensives U.S. Second and Third Divisions entered the line, blocking a German advance toward Paris. For most of this time the Forty-second Division remained miles away, its men almost oblivious to what was going on.

The nature of the German onslaught that dark spring of 1918 has often been described and needs no detailed repetition. Suffice to say that Russia's withdrawal from the war after the Treaty of Brest Litovsk of February 1918 gave the Germans an enormous opportunity, which in retrospect they seized only in part. The Germans should have shifted nearly all of their battle worthy troops to the west, leaving superannuated men who could maintain order in the Russian areas they had occupied. If the German high command had taken advantage of its momentary superiority it could have defeated the British and French before the Americans arrived with enough fresh divisions to make a difference. Instead, the Allies, although nearly overwhelmed by the Germans, stopped the German offensives and held the line. The initial offensive, cunningly planned to divide French and British forces at the place where they joined, nearly succeeded, as it came close to destroying the British Fifth Army and took eighty thousand prisoners. A second offensive opened April 9 farther north and drove a salient into British lines in the vicinity of Armentières. A third began May 27, ten miles northwest of Reims, and reached the Marne in the vicinity of Château-Thierry before being checked by the U.S. Third Division and by the Second Division at Belleau Wood and Vaux, while trucks stood outside the American embassy in Paris in event of the need to evacuate the city.

Through all this turmoil American divisions were arriving in French ports, an astonishing influx that brought the change in Allied fortunes feared by the Germans. Forty thousand men came ashore at St. Nazaire in a single day. Three hundred thousand arrived in France in a single month, May. The British belatedly had offered ships, and the ingenious Americans arranged for men to sleep in shifts, so as to crowd in troops beyond the ships' normal capacities.

Gen. John J. Pershing was slow to turn his divisions over to the French and British, even though at the beginning of the offensives he had promised to do so. Contention has swirled around his stubbornness in seeking his own command, and when the battle of memoirs began after the armistice, critics charged that he risked Allied defeat by attempting to ensure his personal leadership. There was something to the contention, although President Woodrow Wilson wanted the American forces to remain independent and backed him to the hilt, as did his subordinate commanders. Pershing hedged on his promise because he feared Allied commanders, starved for replacements, would brigade American units with their own and employ them as cannon fodder. He determined to establish command over his divisions, creating not merely corps but field armies. By October he managed the First and Second armies with himself as commander-in-chief. By that time the American Expeditionary Forces (AEF) had two million men, a larger force than the British army in France and close to that of the French.

Most of this was unknown to soldiers such as Sherwood. The only thing he knew was that his division while at Baccarat came under direct command of Maj. Gen. Charles T. Menoher, a sign that the Americans would fight under their own leaders.

MAR. 28 One of the great advantages of this place over the front lines is that we get to wash all we desire to. Simply go down to the public fountain and tho it is always cold water it makes one feel good.

We leave in the morning for the front and mounted detail has been ordered to roll its stuff in single packs, in other words, I have to roll all of my belongings into one pack and poor old "Rabbits" has to carry it with me.

I gave the old woman a fine scarf which I will have no further use for and a pair of moccisins which I had extra and she was very happy, but when I told her we were leaving in the morning she seemed quite depressed.

MAR. 29 The so called rest camp is no more. Mounted detail led by Lieut Fisher is off at 8:30 a.m. We rode until noon arriving at Reherry, here we watered and fed our horses, and ourselves ate with an Alabama regiment which is quartered there. Then we went on to our old gun position and got things in shape for the coming of the battery. In evening Smithy and I return to the Echlyon [echelon] which is now situated at Glencourt where we will henceforth stay.

MAR. 30 Rode Rabbits all day investigating telephone lines and putting some in order. Jimmie and I went to Bac in evening. We bought some things including a meal and I got shaved by a woman barber. It is raining cats and dogs.

MAR.
31

This is Easter Sunday, but instead of wearing a new suit etc. I have the one I received in the U.S.A. and look like a tramp. But who cares? not I. Work as usual until noon. In afternoon the battalion is lined up and Major Wainwright presents Kenny [Hughes] and a cook from A Bat the croix deguerre. Our fellows in the Hospital Yates and Fabian will get theirs too.

APR.
1

After the usual routine day Jimmie McArtle and I walked to a neighboring town and found that it was occupied largely by Chinese (laborers). They all had plenty of money and were anxious to buy American tobacco. The French government imports them and pays them comparatively good wages.

APR.
2

Ran a telephone line from battery office to the French central in this town. Ichabod went to hospital accompanied by his boils.

APR.
3

Start of laison detail today with Corp. Smith and Suffle. We are operating projectors in conjunction with battalion headquarters.[1]

APR.
4

We three ride down to Hdq in morning and operate projectors thruout the day. Many nationalities are in the war. Vietnamese— From Anam—Anamites (some good truck drivers[)]—Chinese laborers Russians

APR.
5

Still on projector work signalling and establishing relays from front lines to Hdq.
　　Yesterday within view there were four German sausages and three French observation baloons.[2]
　　Early this morning a big German plane flew over our echlon but was driven away in a short time.

APR.
6

The German offensive (against British lines) which is gaining some ground has not discouraged us in the least because we figure it is his last big bid for victory and it is costing him heavily.

APR.
7

Today the laison detail relayed messages from headquarters to both batteries of the battalion.

APR.
8

Received a box of delicious cakes from Mrs. Scott and a great big box of candy from Aunt Phene today. The Y.M.C.A. has a canteen near us now so that we can get a few luxuries but not so good as those sent over by those at home.

APR.
9

Y.M. gave a movie show in our billet this evening and since we have not seen the movies for a long time, the show was a great success. Of course everyone talked aloud about the pictures giving the characters in the play names of members of the audience and in this way a lot of roasting was done.

National Archives

First Battalion, 150th Field Artillery (formerly First Indiana Field Artillery), signaling airplane from an artillery position, Reherrey, France, 1918. Airplanes gained prominence as reconnaissance craft during World War I, finding enemy positions and directing artillery fire.

APR.
10
The main event of the day in my estimation was the shower bath in *warm* water I got at the infirmary.

APR.
11
Corps Cottingham and Carrol of battalion HQ and I went to R.T. [?] observatory today establishing communication from there to HQ. While we were there a squadron of five Hun planes passed above us.

APR.
12
A year ago today I enlisted and almost half that time has been spent in France. Time has passed swiftly for me.

There was quite a bit of activity on our part today. Both batteries adjusted on German batteries by areoplane observation.

I watched the panel work at HQ this morning, by means of which the areoplane is signalled. Cloth strips are arranged in different positions on the ground by three men, these can be seen by the aviator and by the arrangement he reads the message.

On the other hand his messages are sent to us by wireless. He sees how and where our shells are falling and directs the changes.

APR.
13
Our outfit has tossed over some gas shells in the last twenty-four hours.[3] Today laison detail observed more panel work.

APR.
14
It rained all day and Lieut. Harris called me over to do some secretary work.

APR.
15
YMCA gave a movie show at our billet tonight and since they are so unusual everybody had an uproarious time.

APR.
16
Rained all day detail spent it practicing projector work at Esch.

APR.
17

I was changed from laison to instruments again but will remain at wagon line for present.

APR.
18

The battery has received about fifty new horses now in preparation for enlargement of outfit and we are all kept busy thruout the day, caring for them.

APR.
19

Went to Baccarat today with Lieut Scheffer and detail and brought back six new horses.

Illinois band played last night. Gee it sounded wonderful. The ragtime made us think of home. How they are dancing and having a good time perhaps I should say how we used to—then I could imagine how the boys who are fortunate enough to be in the American army when it returns home victorious after the war will march down 5th Ave or Wash. street behind such a band how the streets will be lined and how proud we will be but I will think all the time of Dad and mother, who will be waiting for me. Then the band played The Star Spangled banner and every man froze into the salute. I know there was not one man in the assembly who would not have been willing to die for his country.[4]

APR.
20

Took a detail to battalion headquarters and dug some trenches for telephone lines. While in town Corp. Cottingham showed us some of his drawings and he surely is a wonder—Has studied at Heron institute Indianapolis.

APR.
21

Pay day—I rode Rabbits to Bac where I bought a money order for $50 which I have sent home.

In this town they were playing baseball and the YMCA was crowded. I also had my picture taken to send to the folks.

APR.
22

Raining harder than usual today and all of our now vast number of horses got a good bath, I believe I should have received the same treatment because my last bath was somewhere in the hazey past.

APR.
23
Rode to battery and went with Sgt. Stolte to O.P.[5] Lieut Barbar gave me a map of our sector and I studied it because I will be called on at times to observe enemy movements.

APR.
24
Rain again but arrival of mail relieved the depression among less important news I find the startling news that I am a god father to Elmer Schloot who has just arrived.

APR.
25
Went with a mounted detail to division Hdq and brought to wagon line, nine new horses.

APR.
26
Lieut Vallandingham, whom I knew at Ft. Harrison has been assigned to Bat. B. in place of Lieut. Gasper who has gone to brigade headquarters.
    Inspection by the major today.

APR.
27
We are doing more night firing than usual now averedging 250 rounds.

APR.
28
On regimental guard having sentries along streets of town and at picket line. A Boche plane made us a visit during the night but he was driven off by the aircraft batteries.

APR.
29
Rabbits and I got leave to _____ and had our pictures taken.[6]
    Henry Sisk of Linton sent to guard house for fighting Sgt Ofie and for drunkenness. Tough luck for him.

APR.
30
The Y sec. Mr. Dabney pulled the biggest entertainment we have seen yet, tonight. It was a Franco American affair and an orchestra from the Illinois band played.
    The French contributed mostly grand opera while we gave some songs and another fellow and I made pretty speeches.

Battery C, 150th Field Artillery (formerly First Indiana Field Artillery), St. Pole, France, May 1, 1918.

MAY
1

At 1:30 today intense cannonading by our batteries began. All caliber guns are taking part including the long rangers.

Several batteries of French have also come to assist us, this being almost exclusively a sector of the Rainbow division before.

MAY
2

An areoplane buzzes above our heads an observation balloon is up to our right and our guns are booming and shaking the earth. I am sitting on the edge of an old trench from which the Germans were driven earlier in the war and there are wooden crosses here and there, some have only the word Allemand painted on them while others have French names with La Patria and the tri color.

But those are only signs of the past. Boche shells are bursting in our territory to remind us of that. But here on the crest of the hill I have a commanding view of the surrounding country and I can tell that the Americans are dropping ten shells into German territory while Fritz honors us with one.

What a beautiful land to be torn by war. Beautiful villages nestling among these Lorrain hills—hills so symettrical. The villages are in ruins but it is spring and in spite of Mars mother nature has covered the hills with verdent growth, the wild flowers are springing up and forests are donning their spring foilage. In the distance are the Vosges rising into the clouds.

And here we are mere men mutilating, scarring, hurting you but for what. After all you beautiful hills and mountains clothed with a cloak of grass and flowers are the creation of the same all powerful force as we—

and this suffering is for us as great as for you. We are destroying you and ourselves for ideals and for principles worthy of him of Nazareth.

Evening is coming on and the flash of the big guns is accentuated. There is a flash and a little smoke pours from the muzzle of the engine of destruction in a few seconds the crash reaches our ears and with my glasses I can see the burst of the high explosive shell in the Boche territory.

We are giving them hell now and if they let our boys loose it will be only a short time until a decision is reached. We will win or die in the attempt and we are confident that we will win. Our blood is up oh why don't they let us show what we can do. Well, the sector has never been so lively since we have been here so perhaps our offensive *is* started.

Ah but the thunder of our guns is music to my ears. There goes a big eight inch there a 75 and there our own six inch howitzers. One can detect the difference by the sound if they don't all fire at once.

When night comes on we are favored with a wonderful electrical display. Never on Saturday night was the main street of the home town so bright nor did any fourth of July celebration ever equal the display over no man's land. The rockets illumine their own brilliant courses and the star shells hang for a moment in the air and while suspend cast a stunning light and brightness surpassing even the daylight.

From a distance it is beautiful and war is romantic; at the guns it is work. The gun crews sweating—their energies and muscles minds and bodies applied to the work of ramming shells into the breach of the cannon pulling the lanyard which releases the firing pin whereupon the projectile is hurled at the enemy. And in the front line trenches the doughboys are anxiously awaiting the signal to go over the top, or are keeping their eyes open to detect any movements in the enemy trenches.

One can scarcely comprehend the magnitude of all this within his view. Yet after all what a small part of the war is this. We can only slightly conceive it much less describe it.

In other ages great authors could vividly describe battles and wars and Victor Hugo gave us a literary gem in his account of the battle of Waterloo; But today even he would despair.

War has not been shorn of romance but its magnitude its mechanics overshadows all else. The charge of the light brigade was a brilliant episode but a charge of six hundred in this war is a minor incident; oh yes Pickett's charge has been duplicated and enlarged in this war but such an incident will take no pages in a history.

Every person in the warring nations are effected by the war. Soldiers are being trained, civilians are contributing their money to war loans and economising on food. Men and women are manufacturing munitions ships etc. The heart of the nation is in the war.

Over here at the ports ships deposit their cargoes of war material all of France is pulsating with war. Agriculture is more important than ever

National Archives

One Hundred Fiftieth Field Artillery (formerly First Indiana Field Artillery), firing barrage at 4:15 A.M., Reherrey, France, May 3, 1918.

manufacturing is vital, vetrans on leave mingle with the old men, the women are children once again.

We go farther into the zone of operations. The shell torn and demolished cities, towns and villages once occupied by the Boche are more active than ever before. Really here is to be seen the greatest activity of the war a beehive of activity. Ambulances whizzing along the roads trucks and passenger cars motorcycles. The roads are congested by horse or motorized artillery and regiments of men and all these arteries of travel leading to the front a few miles distance activity is evident largely in exploding shells the guns are camouflaged and the men are burroughed in the ground so the aircraft and shells have a monopoly on movement.

MAY 3	Intense artillery activity all day. Ohio doughboys went over the top this morning, penetrating to the third line and capturing some prisoners.

MAY 4	Sector at normal again with more bombarding at night than in the day time. A few air battles.

Went with a mounted detail to _____ in search of bugler Fike who has gone AWOL;[7] but were unable to get track of him.

Two real American girls and a mere man entertained us tonight on an imprompter stage. They were good sports and of course the fellows went wild and sang songs with them and whistled. A sight of them was good and

I have a feeling now that I will fall in love with the first girl I see when I get back to God's country.

MAY 5 | Bishop McConnel of Michigan visited us today and spoke. He is a fine fellow and gave us lots of good pointers fact is I have found that the religious workers (Y men chaplins etc) are not only good men; but have an understanding of common men and they are more interested in humans than in creeds.

MAY 6 | Ichabod and I got out the old range finder and BC [?] scope this morning and cleaned them up. Then went out on a hill and observed firing.

MAY 7 | Observed at H hill with Ichabod, Brown, and Lieut Vallondingham, who has just been assigned to our battery. Misty day so visibality did not permit good observation, however we figured our visibal enemy territory to the map.

MAY 8 | Observed H.O.P. [?]—more than usual activity of enemy some troop movement and railroad traffic.

MAY 9 | Was on guard last night and today and observed in evening.

MAY 10 | Cleaned my saddle and prepared for inspection which came in the afternoon.

MAY 11 | Usual observation fine visibality so we had a chance to find all known points on our maps and figure the coordinates. A French infantry sergeant observer was observing near us and he pointed out some inconsistencies in our work and owing to his familiarity with the whole sector he was able to help us in several ways.

MAY 12 Mother's day. Pershing has asked all members of A.E.F. to write to their mothers and the Y has supplied the stationary. Of course it doesn't take a special day to make us think of mother but it is good to have a day like this because it will mean a day of clean thots.

I moved myself and possessions to gun position today and henceforth my bunk will be in the telephone dug out.

I must admit that the change from spacious barn to dug out is a point against sleep for smoke from the stove fills my eyes with smoke and it is stuffy here under the ground but one becomes used to it of course.

MAY 13 I am now the gas non com of the battery temporaraly the BC called me in and said that because I had a basis of chemistry he thot I would be fitted so of course since then my time has been occupied with that work.

As many casualties have been the result of gas as shells in the American army so all precautions are being taken and we are receiving a great deal of equipment including gas proof hats coats and trousers. I also have a crew of four men as a disenfectant squad.

Went to the wagon line with Figgis in the fourgon to get enough horse masks from A Bat to equip the rest of our horses.[8]

I went up to Lieuts. Harris [?] and Scheffer's room to get a book and Lt. Scheffer kept me there until 1 am. talking of everything imaginable from war to religion and reading poetry.

MAY 14 Back at guns—went to battalion headquarters for supplies at noon, and put in a gas proof door in first section dugout.

Battery fired all night. Believe me one has to hand it to the cannoneers for guts because every time a gun is fired the old earth shakes for miles and the sound is terrific except to ones used to it it would be nerve wrecking.

The air vibration is so great that candles refuse to stay lit in any of the dug outs.

MAY 15 Fine spring day. Several of us engaged in a cootie hunt and needless to say were successful in slaying many victims.

We established semaphore communication within the "country club" in afternoon. I washed this evening—a noteworthy event, but it will be a regular occurrence from now on because there is a good pool of water down in the old stone quarry a short distance from the fourth piece.

MAY 16	Two areoplane battles today in each case Boche turned tail. Not long ago our anti-aircraft guns brought a Hun plane down and it landed in "no man's land" the piolet being killed. Our dough-boys went out and stripped the machine of souveneirs and

returned to our trenches just in time for the Boche turned their guns on it and destroyed it.

MAY 17	Usual day of intermittant artillery activity. Received six letters in the mail today.

MAY 18	We were awakened at one a.m. by the horns and others' gas signals. We were not affected by the gas attack but there were casualties in E from it.[9] In the evening Wright and I walked a couple of miles to the Y.M.C.A. but much to our chagrin

it was closed.

MAY 19	Observed with Stalte at T.H. [?] this morning while battery fired. I inspected all the gas blankets and equipment with officers from general staff in evening. Went swimming in old stone quarry in afternoon.

MAY 20	A meteorlogical baloon came down a half mile behind our positions today. Spent day in fixing up gas doors. Went in swimming at quarry.

MAY 21	Our own activity was increased today, but there was more doing in the air three planes of ours met three Boche and one Hun went hurlling to the ground landing just behind the German first lines.

MAY 22	Feature of todays bill was inspection by the major general and Brigadier general of our Division and brigade respectively.

MAY 23 Preparations for leaving are under way and today each man turned in a blanket and boots to be shipped. The general opinion is that we will go back of the lines for a time when each man will get that long expected leave of 7 days.

MAY 24 Front comparatively quiet today and we didn't fire a shell tho the 75s to our left were busy. Fact is we all remarked how much like a camping trip it seemed. We made coca and toast in dugout tonight sang and played cards.

MAY 25 Final inspection before leaving this sector. More activity than usual including aviation our flyers have gained the supremacy in this sector and the Boche seldom venture over us now While a squadrille of ours patrolls their lines often.

MAY 26 Activity increased on front Huns conducted a raid on us today, so we are giving them hell in return.[10]

MAY 27 Our aviators brought down three Huns today in this district. One fell in flames leaving a black streak of smoke in the sky after him. He fell near Bat. A. hence they have lot of souveneirs.[11]

MAY 28 Daggett came out to position this morning to take up the gas work so I move back to echelon. Hun propaganda ballon fell near here and several of us went out and got some of the pamphlets telling how the Deutsche were winning the war.

MAY 29 Second Boche offensive (Spring) has started (yesterday).
Two gas alarms last night so with having my mask on a while and my skin burning with this poison I got no sleep to speak of. Doesnt hurt today however. I washed up my saddle and got saddle bags and bridle together so that I will be ready when ordered to leave. Artillery activity quite intense last night.

| MAY 30 | Memorial day—Alabama band played and a certain Baron who's greatgrandfather was once mayor of Strassburg spoke on why France wanted Alsace Lorraine back and we all hoped we'd meet him in his native country soon. |

| MAY 31 | This _____ wire (fence wire) bed is rotten no springs mattress and only too blankets so with this poisening on my chest and hives and welts all over me + cooties I spend a mighty comfortable night. Rats and cats run hither and thither. |

Plans for our moving to another front seem changed and we are to remain here.

| JUNE 1 | "Dad" Bennet was transferred to engineers Corps today he hated to leave the boys and I was sorry to see my old friend go.
Ichabod and I go to OP and observe our firing. It was a great sight to see the Boche trenches levelled by old battery B. |

| JUNE 2 | On guard today but with it had charge of digging a new Latrine.
French infantry has been passing thru here in a constant stream and as a result of it the battery is tobaccoless. It was good to see the boys give all their treasured hoards of tobacco to the |

comrades. We had just had an issue yesterday so had quite a lot. Ericsson had hoarded more than average today and he showed me his stack with the air of a connisiuer but as all the others he gave it to the Frenchies who hardly knew what good tobac is.

I am again favored with cooties picked off three today so applied cootie powder which burns and is as troublesome as the animule so being between two fires.

| JUNE 3 | Had charge of hauling today and took two wagon loads of water to the gas den. |

| JUNE 4 | A peculiar thing about some of the old Frenchmen is that they wear sashes, it is said for the benefit of their back and kidneys a red one seems especially beneficial. |

JUNE 5

Observed from OP with Ichabod. Bat was calibrating guns so we took the data of the fired shots.

JUNE 6

Hike today of whole battery. Went down near old rest camp.

JUNE 7

Inspection.

JUNE 8

Same old routine day.

JUNE 9

Ditto.

JUNE 10

Went to infirmary this morning and was doped and told by the Md. that I have the trench (3 day) fever.

JUNE 11

Feel rotten and am not doing much work today.
    Quite lucky on mail today receiving ten letters.

JUNE 12

The snow now is that the 150 FA had been detached from the Rainbow division and we will remain in this sector for quite a while yet.
    Feel much better today though somewhat weak.

National Archives

Street scene. Activities behind the lines became routine as divisions waited to be called to the front.

National Archives

Guns and horses of the 151st Field Artillery, waiting to move up to the front. After a lot of "snow" (rumors), Sherwood's division was ordered to the front in June 1918.

JUNE
13
Did signal work at guns today.

JUNE
14
Day at guns in signal work. It rained all day.

JUNE
15
Got "Rabbits" back today. Rode to R— after him, and it surely was a pleasure to get him back.

JUNE
16
Sunday, quiet day.

JUNE
17
Rained all day and during the heaviest downpour we had to ride the horses several miles to "exercise" them. If brains were money some of our _____ would be paupers.

JUNE
18

Several miles, we hiked today. We are leaving this sector soon for the big battle it is said.

JUNE
19

Ichabod and I observed from H today. Left this town for good at 11 pm. and hiked all night.

4 | Espérance-Souain

(JUNE–JULY 1918)

The next assignment for Elmer Sherwood's division brought him and his companions much closer to serious action. On July 5 the Forty-second took up an intermediate position east of Reims behind two French divisions. The Americans sent one brigade to each of the divisional fronts. The fourth German offensive, an attack along the Matz River, a tributary of the Oise, to divert French reserves and widen a local salient, began on June 8 and ended in failure five days later. The last of the great offensives was launched from a salient along the Marne, some distance from the Forty-second. The enemy penetrated only one small part of the position held by the Forty-second and was thrown back on the first day, July 15, with heavy German casualties. In an Allied counterattack on July 18, Sherwood's division had almost no part and was withdrawn.

The artillery of a division, especially the heavy batteries as in Sherwood's regiment, was not likely to encounter heavy casualties because it was behind the infantry lines. But an explosion of one of B Battery's guns brought the war very close. For the rest of Sherwood's service he would find this tragedy impossible to forget.

JUNE 20

Arrived in this burg at 7: am after an all night hike. Slept in morning and then rode horses in afternoon bareback.

JUNE 21

Pay day. Spent day in grazing horses, grooming etc. My old pal Ichabod was busted today with several other non-coms over an affair not their fault. Slept in a real bed tonight and had real home food.

JUNE 22

Bat. left at 9 pm. hiking to _____ where we entrained about 12. Rabbits fought and kicked but we finally got him into the car.

I with the detail went on the battalion train and though we were somewhat crowded in our little box car I slept like a log on the bare floor.

National Archives

Washing horses in a stream. Soldiers were responsible for the care and grooming of their horses. Sherwood was demoted because his horse was injured.

JUNE 23 We spent a pleasant day hanging our feet out the doors of our horse Pullmans and viewing the country.
    We arrived at our destination 7:30 pm. detrained and hiked to our next camp where we arrived at 12 pm.

JUNE 24 Revillee 7:30 took care of our horses and returned to our bunks which we have found to contain plenty of cooties.

JUNE 25 We are supposed to be resting but with horses that is impossible. As the parody goes "Will there be any horses in heaven if there are I don't want to go there?"

JUNE 26 Saw a newspaper this evening for the first time in two weeks and was pleased with the news that the Italians are cleaning up on the Austrians while on the western front the Allies are gaining local successes especially the Americans.

JUNE 27

Washed all harness and wagons in the morning and in afternoon I scrubbed Rabbits and took a hot shower myself.

JUNE 28

Bareback riding in morning. Left this camp at 11 p.m. hiked all night and arrived at _____ 4 a.m.

JUNE 29

Slept all morning after taking care of our horses. Groomed in afternoon. Signed pay roll in afternoon. Cooties are more considerate here than usual.

JUNE 30

Planes are constantly flying above us from an aviation field near here. I wish I had the chance of going up in one.
       Received mail from home today a great blessing to a soldier.

"Old Dutch Cleanser," a 155-mm howitzer. By 1916 artillery dominated combat on the Western Front, and commanders on both sides used heavy guns to pound enemy positions.

JULY
1

Groom all our spare time. Its a wonder the horses have any hair left on them.

However, Colonel [Robert H.] Tyndall paid B Battery this compliment: B Battery is the best firing bat. in the Regt. B. Bat. has the best kept horses in the Regt.

I am in charge of the billets today cleaning etc.

In the evening a patriotic meeting was held because as the chaplin said you can't tell where we will be the 4th. The band played and Lt. Col. Carter made a patriotic speech. When he had finished some guy said "It was the same damned kind of a speech which got me into this damned mess."

JULY
2

Groomed most of day but went bareback riding in the afternoon. In the evening the detail went out for projector signalling and got back to billets at 11 p.m.

Katz and I boxed two rounds this evening. first time I have had the glove on since Coctquedan [Coëtquidan].

JULY
3

This morning Ichabod and I went over to the big French Aviation field two miles from our camp. We wanted to go up but unfortunately no planes were going up this morning.

The machines are wonderful and the soldiers take loving care of them. They are all painted up and have pictures on their sides such as dragons, goats etc. In the same way we name our cannon, such as Old Deutsche Cleaner, Maggie Magee etc.

This afternoon the detail and officers went riding without saddles. We had lots of fun racing climbing all sorts of steep hills, steps etc. and hurdles. Rabbits is a little wonder speedy and obedient but he would not go the high hurdle. I wish I had time to teach him a few things.

JULY
4

This morning we groomed and washed harness. Afternoon a holiday. The band dolled up in towels ect as a circus band, and Bat F and B. played ball. The Y added to the spirit of the occasion by serving red lemonade.

Bat pulled out of camp at 4:30 p.m. Arriving at the new front 4 a.m. During the journey we were favored by an unusual electrical display out on no man's land which reminded us more than ever of the way in which we are spending the nation's anniversary.

JULY
5

This morning we pitched our pup tents (Roddy being my bunkie, two men in a tent you know) in the wood where we strung ropes for picket lines for our horses. This is to be our echlon.

After sleeping four hours I got up and went down to the gun position where the detail strung lines all afternoon and evening.

JULY
——
6

Our battalion has taken a large dugout in rear of the guns (400 yds) and here we have installed the centrals battalion and A and B batteries.[1]

The dug out is about 40 feet beneath the surface so is safe. I was on the board most of the day and in the evening Dan Schwarz, Long, and I ran a line to the Echlon, which was moved to a wood to right of original location.

JULY
——
7

On switch board three hours today and three night.

In the evening I walked over to Regt. hdqs where at the Y. I bought luxuries for the 1st battalion and brought them out in the fourgon wagon.

JULY
——
8

The most exciting thing I did today was to wash my clothes. The sun dried and bleached them in an hour quite a change from the rainy days when it took us weeks to dry them.

The observation balloon which has been located in rear of us was moved forward today, passed along held by a cable to a moving automobile.

JULY
——
9

Each of us was issued a French canteen. They are of greater capacity than ours.

On board as usual and in evening line to posit. went on the blink and Dan and I shot the trouble which was merely the rotten cable we have been using.

JULY
——
10

This morning went with a detail to battalion hdqr. where we reeled three spools of wire. We loaded them on the fourgon and the bunch rode to the Fr. central, where we were to extend it to our new O.P. Dan and I walked running and testing the line already laid which was out of order.

Then we joined the rest of the detail who were running the line. We worked like slaves taking and pulling the line thru barbed wire and trenches.

At 8 p.m. we had taken it to the observers sleeping quarters. Fulkinson came with Fink's mount and Rabbits and we made a speedy ride to the dugout. Then Perry and I took the horses to the Echelon and walked back in a blinding rain.

We reached the dugout soaked and ate our supper (cold). It was 10 p.m. then and we went on the board from 12:30 p.m. to 6:30 a.m. If I had done a days work like this in civilian life walking probably fifteen or twenty miles in all and then stayed up all night wet and tired I would have thought I required a day's rest but [end of entry]

JULY 11 | Today up early, reeled two reels of wire at battalion and went to observer's tent in morning. Ran the line to the O.P. by 6:00 p.m. this time. However, we had a dinner and a cold supper awaited us at the dug out.

JULY 12 | Vernon Brown and Hoenick joined the detail this morning making it number nine men.

I washed all of my dirty clothes and made them white too; the hot sun dried them in a few minutes. What a change from the rainy season when it took weeks to get clothes dry.

We talked to a French infantryman who lived in Paris and talked English fluently. I asked him a question in French and he came back in English. He had just come from Chateau Thiery [illegible] was enthusiastic in his praise of the Marines, whom he thot wonders.

Dan and I walked about three miles and "hit" three canteens before we found one with supplies, when we did find it we bought sardines, milk, coca, and jam all we could carry consequently we are feasting now.

JULY 13 | In afternoon I took a bath rather chilly but though you wouldn't believe it I needed one.

Battery fired for the first time on this front tonight.

JULY 14 | I was on the board tonight when the battery was ordered to fire. The boys sure did raise Cain for a while. Things calmed down and at 10:30 I went to bed but at 11:30 I was awakened by a terrific sounds, which showed that the big battle had commenced.

I never saw or heard anything so intense the battle zone is alive with artillery and it is difficult to distinguish between the bursts of enemy shells and the roar of our guns.[2]

As soon as I woke I ran down to the battery the fourth gun had just blown up and Malcolm and Savio were lying on stretchers. Savio's right leg was practically off and his other badly emaciated. He was being attended to and I went to hold a blanket to shield Malcolm from the wind. The poor boy was unrecognizable. His face was emaciated and burned and he was holding up a stump of an arm. He said, ["]Give em hell boys I guess I can't help any more."

I spoke to him and held the arm putting my finger over the artery from which blood was squirting thus stopping the flow. He said thanks "Doc" old boy. I'm not hurt very badly but it pains some. I only hope that when my time comes I am as game as this little eighteen year old boy.

The medic came soon and I helped him bandage Malcolm up and soon the ambulance came and both were taken to the hospital where they will have a hard fight for life.

Of course I was terribly sorry for him but I didn't have the least feeling of sickness because of the blood, which I thought I would have.

Of course the batterie's firing was not held up at all, by the blowing up of one gun in fact many of the fellows didnt know about it until the ambulance arrived. The explosion was so great that parts of the big gun were found a quarter of a mile away.

I operated the telephone all night, firing orders and messages were constantly coming down and I would transmit them to the captain.

The flashes of the guns were almost blinding and the noise was intense, conversation was difficult. Enemy shells could be heard and not seen which wasn't especially pleasant but I don't think anyone was afraid though one didn't know but that the next minute one would be finis. No man's land was more brilliant than ever if possible flares star shells rockets and roman candles and every where the flashes of artillery.

JULY 15

Morning came with a slight diminution of artillery fire but it was resumed in intensity soon and now we could see where the German shells were lighting ours only in our gun pits but they had circled and hemmed us in perfectly. Roads were being shelled but in spite of it we got coffee bread and butter at about 4 a.m. A little later we put down a barrage behind our own line so the Huns captured three lines evidently. They drove thru the Alabama boys by superior numbers for the gain but they were so infuriated at seeing some of their boys killed that with out orders and with no artillery preparation they recaptured their trenches running the Boche out with Bowie knives (they had run out of ammunition). In fact they went over against orders it is said but this doesn't surprise any of us who know these boys. They don't know what fear is.

The captain says this is the biggest battle in history. The drive being along a front extending from Chateau Therey [Thierry] to Verdun.[3]

This morning at about 10 a.m. I came back to the hill where the dug out is to snatch a little sleep. I had dozed when I was awakened by a crash and my pup tent was sprayed with dirt. I looked out and—if a shell hadn't burst twenty feet from me a scrap of the shell made a hole thru my tent but missed me. Needless to say, I went down into the dug out; slept about an hour and then went on the board for most of the day.

At four I was called to the battery to take care of the line there and stayed until 7 a.m. when I returned to dug out and slept until 7 (best sleep in coons age.)

JULY
16

The firing is not so intense today. Brownie (sgt.) is missing hasnt been seen since day before yesterday when he went forward to get some observing instruments and he never returned. We have a few men out on account of shell shock.

Huns made five attacks on our lines today and were repulsed with fearful losses.

JULY
17

The artillery activity increases at night and since we are in a salient the flashes of the guns light the sky on three of our sides.

One difference between this front and the Lorraine is that the number of areoplanes is so much greater sometimes one can count as high as thirty five up at one time. There are also many observation baloons. Within our view today a French plane went over the Hun lines and brought down a balloon in flames leaving a black smoke streak suspended in the air for a while.

I took the fourgon past the echelon today a[nd] got five large spools of wire in a French camp which has recently been deserted by the French and no wonder they had been an enemy target and though many soldiers who were killed had been removed, there was an awful stench from the stables which had been wrecked filled with dead horses.

Poor old Brownie was killed and is buried with the dead of a French battery. Our chaplain learned this today.

Gas alarms are frequent the doughboys are no doubt drenched in it but we have gotten it only in a diluted form.

The Huns have been driven back from all our trenches and by brilliant work our doughboys have captured the Boche front lines.

The Echlon has been bombed but only three casualties have been reported.

JULY
18

A red cross ambulance brought a paper of yesterdays date to us today and it is full of news about the failure of the German drive. It says that Epernay and Chalons were the Boche objectives and we are in the direct path of the latter. The paper also says that the first eight hours of the battle saw the most intense fighting of the war.

Now the Franco American troops are driving Fritz the other way and west of Reims have made some great advances.

Since the Rainbow division is a shock division we will be moved to the place where the most intense fighting takes place so unless Fritz wakes up here we will probably move soon.

National Archives

An American major in an observation balloon flying near the front lines, 1918. Balloons were used for reconnaissance during the Civil War and World War I. However, it soon became apparent that the more maneuverable airplane was better suited for observation tasks.

The French General of the sector has given the division a citation praising our work and the division has given a report of our activities which certainly makes us all proud of the division.

We have suffered over two thousand casualties it is said but Fritz has paid for it ten fold. One of the Alabama boys brought down a plane with his automatic rifle killing the aviator.

Colonel Tyndall has been awarded the Croix de guerre with palm, and Legion of Honor and another decoration the name of which I have not learned.

We put over a barrage this morning and our boys went over into the Hun lines bringing back a number of prisoners. One of them wanted to see the American machine gun cannon which was only the 75's used by the 149th with such deadly effect. The regt. went up into the third line trenches and fired point blank into the advancing German columns on the15th. causing fearful loss.

JULY 19 | Out on lines all morning. They were all shot to pieces by the Hun fire and were a job to fix. I walked about twenty miles I believe.

About noon Lieut Vallandingham came out to where I was working and said that the battery was moving, so I high tailed in and since Sgt Fink was at the O.P. organized the detail and got in all the wire possible loaded it and got our horses and joined the rear of the column.

The Frenchmen, whose positions were next to ours during the hottest part of the battle were downcast at our leaving they are exceptionally generous in their praises saying that the Americans are the best fighters in the world and all that. Well, we did our darndest and can only say we have equal admiration for them. They fight of course as peppery as if they were in their first.

We stopped for dinner near divisional hdqr. and I saw General Menhour [Charles T. Menoher] our Maj. Gen. He is a fine looking man of large build looking to be about 55 years of age.

Arrived at a camp in a woods in the evening and after putting up picket lines and tending the horses we turned in. Ingram and I spread our blankets in the wood on nice mossy ground and slept fine.

JULY 20 | Today was a day of rest aside from care of the horses. I did a washing, however and took a bath also, water is none too plentiful here but at that more than at any place on the front thus far.

We received mail and I got six letters so this evening I am going to answer some of them.

It rained all night and Ichabod and I were soaked. Noticed some farming hereabouts and found as in Lorraine that it was all American machinery mostly Deering implements.

JULY
21

The papers today were full of the news of the Allied drive between the Aisne and Marne. The Americans are especially successful and no doubt the news of their doings will strike fear in the hearts of all the Boches.

At 3:30 Lieut. Hargett, Fultz, Dan, and I went to Chalons and after seeing about the batteries' loading I returned to the battery and led the column to the loading platform. It was dusk and just as we had finished loading the anti-aircraft guns opened up on a Boche raider. It seemed like the front with so much noise and light but the raider was evidently driven back no bombs fell near us.

JULY
22

This night we slept thru soundly on the floor and woke up as we were passing through Troyes. We travelled slowly and made frequent stops. At the station we saw Aussies, Tommy's, and Scots. The people along the way and at the stops cheered us and waved and when we came into the outskirts of Paris one would have thought it a celebration. Every one is so enthusiastic they regard the Americans as their saviors and seem to think them the best soldiers ever. Their spirit surely made us more eger and determined than ever. They reminded me of the journey from Fort Harrison to Camp Mills when everybody greeted our train with cheers and flag waving.[4]

Arrived in evening at Lizy and detrained. In the process "Rabbits" was severely bruised; but not knowing this I rode ahead with Lieut Hargett and Dan Smith and we rode into _____ where we were to billet. The battery followed and we were occupied with the parking of wagons and guns and the picketting of horses until [sentence continues in next entry]

JULY
23

7:30 a.m. when we rolled in for sleep. Rabbits has gone to the hospital and it will be at least two weeks before his bruise is healed. I am blamed for it and will be busted to pvt I presume.

500 prisoners passed thru here this morning. Our troops are still advancing. We are to relieve the 26th division I hear.

This afternoon Roddy and I went through the catholic church of the town. Everything is left in it and Roddy explained what all the priests robes were for and etc.

JULY
24

We have been living on almost nothing for the past two weeks but supplies have arrived and we are now getting good meals ie for dinner boiled beef string beans new potatoes, coffee—bread + butter.

I was called over to Rgt. headquarters this afternoon and who was there but Congressman Bland. He was a welcome sight in his U.S. clothes and straw hat and I had plenty of questions to fire at him about the folks Linton and U.S. His news is all good aireoplane and machine production at the top notch and men coming over 250,000 per month.[5]

I gave him a German coin with the Kaiser's head on it to give to Dad as he has often expressed the desire of having the Kaiser's head. I had thought I would spend it in Berlin but [end of entry].

5 | Aisne-Marne Offensive
(JULY–AUGUST 1918)

Failure of the German effort to push south from the Marne salient, followed by an Allied counterattack that threatened communications within the salient, forced the Germans to evacuate the area and withdraw to the Vesle River on August 1–2. German forces sought to withdraw slowly and thereby fortify the new line. The Allies needed to apply pressure on the German lines to stop this tactic, and the Forty-second Division played a signal part in this venture.

JULY 25 As we were lining up for breakfast we received the order to hitch and form in column. The regiment moved out at nine. After going through a town we took the national road to Chateau Therey [Thierry] pressing along this road was a continuous line of traffic mostly trucks and to my surprise most of the trucks coming from were driven by Annamites (resemble Chinese), who come from Anam a protectorate of France.

All along the road could be seen signs of the recent battles for only in the last month have the Germans been driven from this territory. The woods bore the most marks of battle, here and there were boxes of ammunition and shells most of them German.

Hastily dug trenches were every where and fields of grain were likewise scarred. Going farther we saw the bodies of dead Huns and horses in fact the odor of dead things permeated the atmosphere every where.

Had supper in the streets of Chateau Therey. Watered our horses in the Marne at the place where the Franco Americans drove the Huns back a few days ago. The bridge here is destroyed but is being rebuilt by the Americans. The city is not so damaged as one would think because both sides were moving their artillery at this point Franco-Americans forward and Boches back, but all the houses are scarred with rifle and machine gun bullets.

Trenches are dug in some of the streets and other signs of the conflict are every where in evidence; there are three German cannon (77) in the square and open front stoops show that the Germans have rifled them as

17672

National Archives

One Hundred Fiftieth Field Artillery, passing through Château-Thierry on its way to the front to relieve the Twenty-sixth Division, July 25, 1918. The scars of war were obvious in Château-Thierry and its environs.

well as the homes here, evidence of this is seen along the path of the retreating Germans I saw three high silk hats frock coats and such along with discarded German uniforms.

After supper our column took the national highway which is more congested with traffic than any road I ever saw supply trains and troops moving forward, to the rear ambulances filled with wounded, some even sitting on the running board, troops moving back from the line.

We passed through a town destroyed by artillery fire the worst mess I ever saw not a building standing, just piles of brick and fragments.

Arrived at new echelon ten p.m. and the detail immediately set out running lines. It was morning when I returned to the echelon. There are more Americans along this immediate front than French in fact the secor is American and held by the 26 28 and 42 divisions.

On every hand we were asked who we were by passing troops and when we would answer 42d they would all say "Oh Rainbows" they all know us, and from their remark thought us a fine bunch.

JULY 26 We will pull into position tonight. Today we took up some lines and in passing through the woods which dot the landscape here I have seen more evidence than ever of the week's battles. Trenches zig zag crazy courses through them and everywhere is ammunition shells from the largest big gun size to rifle amm. Clothing and German helmets are every where. One thing is certain souvenier hunters will find plenty after the war because it would be almost impossible to gather all of this salvage.

Wooden crosses mark the graves of numberless American, French and German dead but time has not permitted the diggers to get them all yet and I have seen many still lying upon the ground. The intensity of the fighting can be judged by the number of dead in the vicinity. Certain difficult hills have cost us a great price but there are as many Germans dead as ours. It is all in war of course—but even looking upon a dead German I have to be sorry that he was led into such folly as fighting for the Kaiser, and they are human, though some of the things they do seem to mark them as savages and beasts for instance we have picked up German rifles with the saw toothed bayonets attached. The use of these alone mark them as dirty cowards.

I saw an American today lying there and one of his legs was fifty feet away. A German with half his face blown away lay there black now and rotting with maggots pouring from his wounds and in his discarded coat was found his picture as he had once been, a big fine looking youngster pictures of his folks were there too. Could any thing be more terrible? but it is common these days.

We moved into position tonight in a down pour. We worked all night.

JULY 27 Slept some this morning. Battery received ammunition in afternoon. I have talked to some doughboys from the front lines. Three fellows asked where they could find a kitchen had had nothing but a box of hard tack for four days. Their capt and two lieutenants were killed and ninety percent of their company had been put out of action.

Their stories are all the same we are winning a noble victory but with our best blood. It is open warfare every man for himself out there. The Germans have the advantage of being on the defensive and they use their machine guns almost exclusively raking the fields with them but we are always advancing and destroying them.

Our artillery has difficulty in keeping up with the advance but we make short work of the machine gun nests when we get up. Of the 75 batteries sometimes a gypsie gun (single) is sent up with the infantry and it fires into the Boche positions.

JULY
——
28

Bat moved up in column with entire brigade, to new position. The road was conjested and it took us all night to get to the posit. When we reached there guns were swung into place telephone lines were laid and we began firing. I never saw such concentration of artillery even on the Champagne front. All day more has been moving up.

Today we were heavily shelled. To rear of our position a wagon was standing and one of the horses was struck two men were killed and one wounded (A. Bat.). Three horses killed. Our escape seemed miraculous they seemed to hit "where we aint." I was showered with dirt once and shrapnel fell all around but none of our battery was hurt. We have kept up pouring shells into Fritz. We are using two new Deutsche machine guns now which some of the boys found and by the irony of fate they are of American invention, Maxims.

Areoplanes are thick at times overhead. Our fellows have the best of it but once in a while a Carp [?] gets over. One got over today and turned his machine guns loose on E. bat killing two men I hear.

An American won a pretty victory though this afternoon bringing down a Boche in our lines.[1]

JULY
——
29

Was on battalion switch board in an old house on the hill part of last night and slept on an old stretcher I found the rest of the night. Aside from gas alarms we were not troubled.

This morning without breakfast we moved forward about four kilos. At several points roads and woods were being shelled and we were delayed but by noon had pulled into the new position. Swarms of Hun areoplanes come scouting over us it seems that they have the upper hand in the air sometimes they turn their machine guns loose on us and lay eggs bomb but they have not done much damage.

Our fire is not stopped except at times by lack of ammunition. This lack being caused by our moving forward so fast and difficulties of transportation over the congested roads.

JULY
——
30

This has been quite an exciting day. I was out this morning repairing battalion line which was shot up last night, and I had about half a dozen shells burst in my path not far away.

Upon returning to the gun position we made a dive for cover in the small ditches we had dug for protection, because the Hun planes had located us and had directed artillery fire to us. HE's were bursting all about us. At the beginning a caisson was moving from the first gun where it had unloaded its shells, and Corp. Whitfield single mounted was directing it when a shell burst beneath him killing the horse and a piece going up his leg to his back wounding him severely but he will recover. Louie Island was slightly wounded.

Traffic jam. Congested roads were a common occurrence behind the American lines as brigades moved into position.

When I ducked into the trench I happened to have a "Life" in my pocket and during the following bombardment I read it. Believe me shells bursting and singing about make one feel lonesome and I was glad to have something to take my mind off it.

Aside from knocking the bottom out of the water bag and a few funny stunts no harm was done.

In evening we ran an OP line. I operated at O.P. where we had a commanding view of the battle area. It is a great wide valley thru which runs the River Orque. We captured the north bank of it today. Boche as well as our shells are raking the valley.

JULY
31

In the shelling today Fritz killed five of our horses on the picket line in the wood in front of us. Many of our infantry camping near there were killed and the wounded are being brought back on stretchers to our red cross station constantly. Along the main road many bodies of Yanks are strewn some sitting up against trees in natural attitudes. A detail is burying them today.

Five Boches came over us today and dropped bombs. We could see the bombs falling and exploding but the planes were unmolested while doing their dirty work, our planes seem sadly outnumbered, and that doesn't make a fellow feel any more contented when the bombers come over and do as they please. However when they get bold and swoop down on us we have our fun. Our four machine guns including the two Hun guns open up and all of us grab our guns and bang away. I used a German rifel (Brown's) today when one came over low, and blamed if we didn't wing him and bring him down. A captain and private were its occupants both wounded. They were taken back to information.

AUG.
1

Last night I heard an explosion and zowie I was showered with dirt. We made a dive for the trench and passed the night there under shell fire. The attack upon our infantry and bombardment was a demonstration to cover their retreat. We captured Fere-en-Tories [Tardenois].

The prettiest air battle I ever saw happened right over our position. Today seven Huns flew over us dropping bombs and smoke bombs which showed the German batteries our location. A Frenchman came along and picked one Carp out of this bunch driving him downward. There was manouvering. The Frenchman turned a flip clear around the Hun riddling him with bullets, the Hun came down in a spiral nose dive until we could see the pilot and he was close enough to hit with a stone. Of course our machine guns and rifles opened up on him and he lit in a field in front of us. I ran like _____ and was among the first to reach the fallen machine. The lone pilot wounded in head and arm was taken into a nearby house and given first aid. Americans crowded the room and he was scared stiff and begged for his life. We hate them bad enough but couldnt be so dirty as killing a wounded man. I tore off a part of the black cross from the wing of the plane and am going to send it home.

AUG.
2

Moved forward today about five kilos in heavy rain. Along the road we were hungry as everything and as luck would have it we came across an overturned bread cart and I got a whole loaf.

In the distance we see smoking powder dumps and burning towns signs of the Hun retreat. At midnight pulled into position. I managed to get four hours sleep after going on switch board.

AUG.
3

In morning some of the boys went over to an old building and found a lot of German equipment including towels made of paper fabric. We also appropriated several trench periscopes. We are already using three of the Hun carts.

Moved this morning passing through Fère-en-Tardenois. The town is badly wrecked with great piles of debris and masonry everywhere. The town underwent three days of almost constant shelling from our guns.

In some of the fields along the way were many bodies of soldiers mostly Americans with simply a coat thrown over them and a bayonet stuck in front of them. Upon one hill there were hundreds of bodies.

Everywhere one can see where the doughs have dug into banks for protection. We pulled into a wood and had supper. We have nothing to eat but corn wooly. Not even hard tack. We are moving so fast they cant get the supplies up.

Under cover of night we pulled guns into position in a wood and ran our lines. I rolled in at 2. Shells burst around us all night.

AUG. 4

Moved again, this time putting guns into an open field and the SW [?] we put into a gully nearby.

Along with running lines cooties and hives I am pretty active.

Sitting at the board tonight I have time to count the Hun shells as they pass over. They are now bursting in the wood behind us (2 a minute). Here one comes in the distance it seems lazy but closer it meows like a cat and then screams and finally bursts. With my watch I can tell when one will come over when it will burst, etc because they are so regular.

AUG. 5

A year ago today the Rgt was mustered into federal service and mobolized at Ft. Harrison and wonder of wonders today Roddy is starting back to the states as an instructor. I gave him a piece of an areoplane wing to give to Dad as a souvenier.

We received more ammunition tonight.

AUG. 6

We have captured Fismes, Lt. Bennet says. It is tough to be fighting here and not know anything but what happens right here. Once in a while we find a paper the last one I saw was Aug 2 and everything points to German defeat.

AUG. 7

German planes brought down two observation ballons in flames today. The observers managed to get down in their parchutes.

Went up with the captain today and observed firing of the battery.

AUG. 8

Artillery of 13th [Third] div has drawn up alongside us and prospects are that we will be relieved soon. Around Amiens the Boche has retreated the British meeting no resistance in a 30 kilo advance. Great news?[2]

Ran an extended OP line today.

AUG.
9

Spent most of day with telephone in shell hole behind guns getting the dope from our observatory.

We were sniping all day, picking Deutsch off wherever we could see them. Our best hit was two trucks which we blew to smithereens.

The nights are the hell because that is when the Carps always shell us and the singing of shells coming over when you can't see where they hit is not pleasant. They landed all around us and naturally spoiled our sleep. We also had a light gas attack. Moral if you want to sleep try to do it in the day time.[3]

AUG.
10

Allied planes have so increased in the last few days that we have entirely the best of the air battles. Often fourteen fly in one bunch and at times the swarms in the air come in contact with the enemy and the flying and manouevering are almost funny they seem to be playing until one comes down in flames then we realize it is a death struggle.

Today all we have eaten is dried peaches bacon and coffee, and not enough of that.

AUG.
11

Left position midnight and hiked until six when we pulled into our former echelon, but we stayed there only long enough to feed and water the horses then moved on to another wood five kilos farther where we spent the day.

I went over to Bouvardae to the commissary where I bought a pound of chocolates and ate half of them of course I was sick later.

We pulled out in the evening, hiking to Epieds or rather to a wood nearby.[4]

AUG.
12

This is a fine place a stream runs through the wood and our bunks on the grass are very comfortable.

We got new clothes today and you can bet that I was glad to get rid of my tattered torn dirty and cootiefied clothes and take a bath donning my new outfit. Washed saddles, groomed.[5]

AUG.
13

Grazed horses this morning. Fisher, Marsh and I went over to the massive Big Bertha emplacement left by the Huns in their retreat. It is a high affair having over a hundred ball bearings each larger than a man's head. An idea of its size may be gained by knowing that a standard gauge rail road runs thru it and one runs on each side of it.

The gun is [sketch] gone but it is said to have been brought up to the position on five flat cars. The tops of trees about the emplacement are burned showing where the gun had fired.[6]

During our absence the battery moved across the road to another wood and we then were put on extra fatigue, building a bridge, for going over to the gun. The capt claims that orders were read telling us not to leave camp but we and others I have asked didn't hear such a thing but such is this man's army.

AUG.
14

Rotten hot hike of fifteen kilos today. We were ordered to wear gas masks helmets and coats and carry side arms and rifles for those who walked especially this was terrible. But if the fellows attempted to ride wagons or off horses they were ordered off by officers. We finished the hike any way pulling into another wood 5 kilos south of Ch.Th.

In coming through the streets of Chateau Thierry, I see Earl Myers from home. He was looking for me along the column, and of course I was mighty glad to see him and converse for a few minutes about the home town.

AUG.
16

Hiked 7 kilos today, arriving at a big chateau close to Lizzy. In the night Boche planes flew over and bombed the railroad station.

AUG.
15

Hiked 10 kilos to wood near Dhuizy.

AUG.
17

Hiked to Lizzy (2 kilos) and entrained this morning eating dinner on the loading platform. The side door pullman was comfortable since there were only eight of us in the car.[7]

AUG.
18

This morning came through Dormans, Chalons and Epernay arriving at station where we unloaded in the evening. Hiked 8 kilos arriving in Bessancourt tonight.

All the natives were out to greet us. They are very polite and offered their guest rooms to us but only the officers and sergeants were allowed to occupy them by the battery commander.

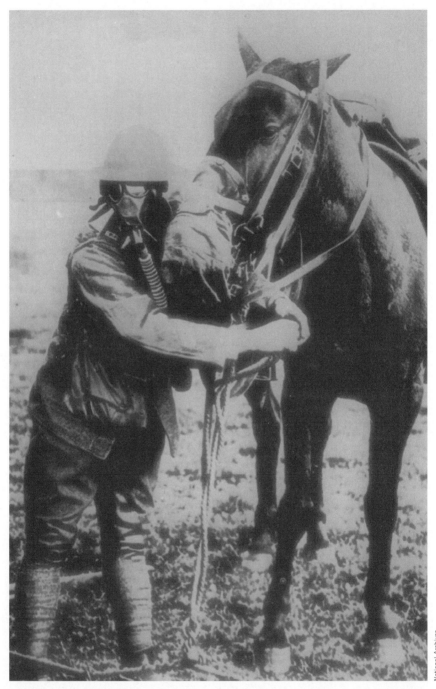

Soldier and horse in gas masks. The gas mask, although cumbersome, was a vital piece of equipment for the World War I soldier, protecting him from poison gas.

AUG. 19 The detail occupies a large room and we have straw to sleep on. In a front room there is a big grate and a pump with wash basin so now we can wash to our hearts content.

I washed all my clothes today and had a bath in warm water second time in a couple of months.

There is boco milk around here and I have it morning noon and night. At noon, fifteen of us went down to the town mayor's house for dinner most I have eaten since leaving home. Two geese potatoes beans cucumbers etc in fact I ate too and enough to last me for a year it feels.

AUG. 20 Inspection of equipment this morning, horses to take care of as usual but had time to write a few letters.

Band gave a concert in front of the town hall this evening and the natives as well as soldiers congregated there.

Peasants with their rakes just in from the fields, a few (2) men in city clothes, dressed up people and dirty ones the old priest and soldiers made quite a picture.

AUG. 21 Quiet day in this dead village aside from caring for horses and sweeping the streets. I like this deadness for a rest camp because we can rest a little but we hear that the silence is going to be broken and we are going to begin drilling soon also that we do not get those long overdue (10 day) passes.

AUG. 22 "Nothing new to report from the grave yard." ["]La Petite Journal" tells today about the great advance of the British and French. It certainly does look fine.

AUG. 23 We ran lines to a French central today from which we get communications with hdq, and we have to keep a man on the board at all times my relief was from 3 to 6 today.

AUG. 24 Part of the day on switch board which is in one of the village homes. I had quite a nice afternoon talking with madame and mademoselle.

I looked through some old files of "La Petite Journal" for 1893 and found some interesting things such as a picture of the Chicago World's fair, an account of a duel which [Georges] Clèmenceau had had, and a cartoon advocating universal equal suffrage, other pictures showed the love of the French for military display and their hatred of the Germans.

Our meals are worse than ever so we buy cheese and milk to live on with an occasional meal with the French people.

AUG. 25 Sunday never was a day of rest in the artillery where the officers are so solicitous about keeping the men busy from morning to night.

Dan, Lavoie, and I had dinner with the family at the telephone central. The rabbit was fine. One of our horses was shot today and while we were at the table some one brought over a steak from it. They think it quite funny that Americans do not eat it.

The people had some sort of a church holiday today. The procession came down the street to a house where the old priest in white robe chanted the service as the boys swung the incense pots. The people carried banners and some sort of symbols.

AUG. 26 New schedule began today revillee 5:15 retreat 6:30 and constant action between including such ancient institutions as squads right.[8] It surely is the intensive training stuff and at a place where we thought we were to rest, seems they think we are still rookies.

AUG. 27 Squads right is not so bad as I thot sort of fun a brushing up. Rode Kennie's pacer [horse] to Battalion tonight to get morning report.

AUG. 28 Practice hike today 7 am to 7 p.m. At noon we stopped in the road near where the Alabama boys were stationed. They told us stories of their adventures and I got a watch and German belt from one of them.

Orders came down this evening and we left Bassancourt at 8 p.m. hiking all night.

AUG. 29 Spent day in Roubecourt hiked all night.

AUG. 30 Day in Bulgneville where some Britishers are stationed. It was the first time I had talked to Britishers much and I certainly was surprised at their generosity of praise for us.

One man over 45 yrs of age said to me ["]Sonny if you boys hadnt come over the Germans would have had both London and Paris by now." He was from Middlesex near London.

Another said that aside from the flying end we had the best army in Europe. They were RFC's[9] and told of many daring things the young American cadets would do.

I congratulated one Britisher on the fine work the army was doing in this drive and he said "well you made us ashamed of ourselves." All of these expressions surprised me for I had heard the English were big headed and gave no one credit but themselves.

AUG. 31 Arrived Landaville 1 am. Staying all day and night here. This evening I went down to see the F battery boys. Sam and Minny I met first and then Nig. Ingram went with me he has just returned from Paris and had a lot to tell.

SEPT. 1 General [John J.] Pershing was expected to come today, so we have been cleaning guns and carriges, but he didn't show up.

SEPT. 2 A vaudeville troupe from the states gave us an enjoyable entertainment tonight.

SEPT. 3 Nig, Pug, Dick, Perry and I had a Beta[10] supper tonight and enjoyed getting together again.

SEPT. 4 Grim and I went to Chatenois today in a truck and were coated with dust when we returned. Leaving tonight—passed through Neuf Chateau at midnight so we are not such a great distance from the front, for which we are surely headed. No smoking is allowed, gas masks must always be worn as well as the steel derbies—like old times? but on the square everybody is happy. We know that when on the front we are doing good helping win the war and believe me when the Rainbows get in there is always something doing. I know we are going to make them turn tail this time just as they did before Chateau-Thierry. Knock on wood Buddy.

SEPT. 5 | Day spent in wood a few kilos out of Neuf Chateau. It rained last night and most of morning but Grim and I were wise and pitched the pup the minute we came into the wood so we are dry. Left this evening for the longest hike we ever took something over 30 kilos. It seems a forced march and we must be needed at the front immediately for it is very hard on the horses and men. I walked aside from the time I relieved lead driver on the escort, but one had to keep moving or freeze. Another wood this morning.

SEPT. 6 | More rain. Rabbits is perfectly well again and was given back to me today so we went on the reconnaisence detail of the Battalion. Starting as the sun was setting and riding till sun rise when we chose the wood we were to occupy.

SEPT. 7 | The column came later and we guided them in. An escort and piece had been ditched and I rode back five miles and brought them in, after which we ate breakfast and then slept until noon when we ate and curried fed watered horses. At 8 p.m. we left camp, moving to the front in the blackest night I ever remember.

6 St.-Mihiel

(SEPTEMBER–OCTOBER 1918)

The American attack on the large German salient to the east of Verdun that contained the town of St.-Mihiel constituted the first major action of the American Expeditionary Forces (AEF), and Gen. John J. Pershing took every precaution necessary for victory. He brought in four divisions, which he had been strengthening throughout the summer and autumn of 1917, and in advance of "going over the top" made preparation for a huge barrage by the First Army's artillery and a sizable body of batteries under French command. Pershing knew that Gen. Ferdinand Foch, the Allied commander ever since the initial German offensive in March, would be watching the performance of his men and did not want anything to go amiss. Nothing did. Indeed when the battle opened on September 12 it was virtually over the next day. German troops had begun to move out of the salient, for the high command desired to shorten the lines of its forces and if possible discover enough troops to transfer some of them to the British front where there had been a near breakthrough on August 8.

And so St.-Mihiel was not much of a fight. Nominally it continued until American occupation of the entire salient on September 16. The only German casualties of moment—there were few on the AEF's side—came from American shelling of troops on roads leading out of the salient, which the artillery barrage naturally focused upon, catching men and vehicles on their way north to what German commanders thought would be safer and easier defense positions.

An awkwardness of St.-Mihiel may well have been that the battle was too easy, emboldening the Americans to believe they had bested the Germans in a full-scale battle, rather than as some wags claimed, that they had relieved the Germans. As compared to the brutal battle of the Meuse-Argonne that followed, St.-Mihiel was an engagement of little consequence.

Another awkwardness of St.-Mihiel was that the American commander-in-chief, seeking to be sure of his first large victory, put too many of his more experienced divisions into the fight. Pershing could have rolled up the salient with second-line troops. Only ten days separated the two battles, not enough time to transfer the divisions, and he began the Meuse-Argonne with mostly green units, men and commanders who never had been in combat.

SEPT.
8

It is 10:30 pm. and I am operating the switch board (seems sort a good to be at the same old stand after our miscalled rest.) I have just had a feed here on the table before me peaches and hard tack and it was a feast believe me because we haven't had much of anything to eat at the battery today. The peaches I bought at a British comissary at Bulgneville over a week ago and I have carried them in my roll ever since. The hard tack is another story. It is (pisened). When we were running a line to our observation post today we came across a shed in which was a big lot of canned stuff upon investigation we found it to be corn woolie and hard tack and being half-starved we broke open some of each and ate there of some guy out of the seven hundred and [—] came up and was horrified to witness our indulgence for said he "That food is condemned" on acct of being dosed with gas.

Jonny Bosson Bat A. spoke up and said Boy howdie gas eating is my favorite indoor sport beside I ain't had nothing to eat for twenty four hours and I'm no Jesus I cant take the piece of hard bread tack they issue me at meal time and multiply it many fold. Well I asked him if it was mustard gas because I always like mustard on my meat anyway.

I brought back a shirt full of the tin boxes of hard tack and they cant starve me now if they try.

After hiking all night we pulled into this position at about 2:30 a.m. and we worked at camouflaging and putting in lines and putting in the guns until about 5:00 then we turned in and slept to 8:30, and that is all the sleep I have had because I have been on the jump all day; but we can go to bed with a clear conscience because all of our lines are in and in good shape.

This evening we ran the line to the O.P. just back of the doughboys trenches. I went down in the trenches and first man I came onto was a draft I asked him how far the german lines were and he didn't know said he thought they were over there. I asked him if there was much excitement and he said a fellow out of G co was killed by a shell last night. He seemed to think it quite a bloody war what he would have thot had he seen the fields before Chateau Thierry covered with dead I don't know.

Well, its dead as a door nail around here now but we sure will wake them up soon. Tonight the last of our brigade moved in and we'll be ready to give 'em hell soon. Oh boy won't that be a grand and glorious feeling to get the damned Huns on the run again. The British and French are doing so well that I actually think it possible for the good old US army to deliver the knock out within three months of course it isn't probable but believe me when we have such doughs as the Alabamans who swear they will take Metz if ordered to or die we have to be happy and confident.

SEPT. 9 Ran line to kitchen this morning and repaired battalion line. Our peace is not disturbed by the Boche in fact there is very little activity (The calm preceeding the storm) The guards make you go about with mask at the alerte can you beat that. I asked some guy, a draft if anybody had been gassed on this front and he said in a terrible voice two or three and he added that a man had been hit by a shell yesterday. I told him that it must be an awful hot front that I didnt imagine war was so hellish. These new outfits are alright considering that they have just arrived and havent had much training, they make one sore when the[y] complain about the army life when it has been easy for them in the states, but we will rely on them to show the old American spirit when the time comes.

SEPT. 10 It has been raining cats and dogs today and our dug out leaks badly. The salvation army is located here and we sure have to hand it to them for doing their duty. they lay the YMCA in the shade; this morning they put out hundreds of pancakes coffee and syrup (free) it was the first we had had in many moons and they were fine. The SA does this sort of stuff all the time and they are not run by highly paid secretary's like the YM'ers but by common fellows who volunteer for nothing. A major in the line had no mess kit so he took the flap jacks in his hat.[1]

The first division (Black snake) is here and I have talked to some of them (pretty nice to wear two service stripes). They were the first over, the artillery beating us by three months. We were the third division in France the second being the 26th (Yankee division) Ng's from Mass who preceded us by three weeks, so we were among the first 75,000 and have fought as many days on the front as any division in France not excluding these two. The 1st boys are good fellows and are not the grumbling kind. tho they have seen as many hardships or more than any Ya[n]kees. One fellow wrote on a wall the fronts they had been on and dates and ended Metz 1918 (Sept) Hoboken (1919).

It is said that a Hun prisoner said the Germans only feared two divisions in the American army 42d [First] and the Rainbow the first at Lorraine and Champagne made them look sick and the latter at Chateau Thierry lambasted the Prussian guard to a frazzle. It does look as if the 42d relieves the Rainbow [First] from the amount of line duty we have served.

SEPT. 11 Boco ammunition arrived and we are all set. Worked all day in preparation for the drive, and 1 a.m. we opened up with a fierce barrage. The Hun artillery reply was feeble.

IHS, Bretzman Collection

Marshal Ferdinand Foch, commander in chief of the allied forces. Foch was considered the most brilliant and aggressive of the French commanders.

SEPT. 12 Doughs went over at 5 am. and prisoners are streaming back. They didn't wait for the slow tanks[.]

SEPT. 13 On road all night but battery could make no headway. We got almost to Seicheprey by inches and decided that we could do no good so at day break we turned back and made camp in a wood amidst the old American lines.

SEPT. 14 In wood today. The roads which lead across no man's land are being made passable but for the present traffic is being held up.[2] This is the first front where we have undoubtedly had supremacy of the air. We have boco planes here.

SEPT. 15 Am writing this at 2 a.m. having just got communications with P.C. Battalion and guns.[3] The gun crews finished camoufladging at 1 am. and the chow wagon brought us our delayed supper at that time. Even hard tack and corn wollie tasted good.

Our switch board is in a shack with five bunks in it. The Huns had made this wood into a rest camp and even had electric lights. Among other Deutch stuff I found a propaganda paper published by them but in French entitled "Gazette Des Ardennes." It is illustrated with cartoons of "Rotten John Bull" and high cost of living etc calculated to cause discontent among French readers.

Went to Pannes on Rabbits in afternoon after working on lines all morning. Walked up by a general's car as it pulled out asked a dough if it were General Pershing for though I didn't get a good view I thot it was and the dough said it was, that he had seen him several times today.

SEPT. 16 Read a propaganda paper today entitled America in Europe and published at Hamburg. It intends to cause dissention in the American ranks but is considered quite a joke among us.

The Austrians have made proposals to the allies for a conference to discuss peace but of course it is impossible for us to discuss anything with the pirates when peace comes it will be dictated by us.

SEPT. 17 At O.P.[4] today saw an american plane bring down a Boche.

Tonight we were (favored) with an air raid we heard the planes above and then the crash when the bomb exploded. C lost two men.

Went out on an expedition this afternoon and got a German helmet and gas mask which I intend to send home.

SEPT. 18 No change in the general situation in this sector and the doughs are digging in. The Boche is bringing up more artillery and activity in this respect has somewhat increased but we are far superior in this respect to him.

Ran OP line today. The OP is on a platform in the top of a very high tree and was made by the Huns. It is a very fine OP having a commanding view of the enemy territory for miles. We fired on several targets during the day while observation was perfect. Field Daily was adjusting for second battalion and with Lt Chambers of D and Pete Straub of A all in the OP we had several discussions about IU [Indiana University].

Ichabod and I went over to Beney, and ransacking through the houses which had been, until the drive, occupied by the Huns, we found several souvenirs I got a picture of [Field Marshal Paul von] Hindenburg and a few trinkets. While there the town was shelled, two men being killed in a house a short way down the street. Some of D battery were pulling out of town one of the big 8 in Krupp rifles which the Rainbows captured (painted 42 div. Booty) and they are going to fire it and possibly some of the other guns which are there one of which is a Russian piece.

After dark a small party of us went back from our position to Beney and carried back two milk cans of hot chocolate from the Y.M.

Tonight the Huns are throwing over quite a number of gas shells and toward morning they put on a heavy barrage.

SEPT. 19 Pete Sefton, who bunked next to me in old Co. L.T.C. came over today. He is 1st Lt. in the 168 infantry of our division, has been gassed and is quite enthusiastic about hunting Huns. Grim found a sack of flour in Beney left by the Boche and conse-quently we had pancakes for breakfast and biscuits for supper.

SEPT. 20 Grim, Campbell and I went to Beney this afternoon and got some Y.M. supplies for the battery. We also went to a German garden and dug three sacks of potatoes sack of cabbage and basket of beans and brought them back to the kitchen on a cart which we found. The YMCA secretaries on this front are hard workers and I have changed my opinion of them as a class. We tore up a Hun town today.

SEPT. 21 Our firing averages about the same each day limited by lack of ammunition but we put more shells over than Fritz can. Our tar-get yesterday was a village within his lines and being on a promi-nent hill it was within plain view of our guns. The falling walls and smoke of bursting shells was a long to be remembered sight. We were paid (for 2 mos) today and Paul O'neil and I collected money from each man for the purpose of getting an orphan for the battery's adoption. The plan is through "the Stars and Stripes" and we turn over money for the support and schooling of a French war orphan for one year.[5]

SEPT. 22 | I am suffering from some kind of an itch which covers my body and with a combination of fleas, cooties, and hives my nights are not spent in dreaming pleasant dreams.

SEPT. 23 | We fired more than usual last night the occasion being a raid in which our boys took 16 prisoners. Our fighting is limited to this kind of action. Grim promoted some rabbits and a chicken so we expect a feast soon.

SEPT. 24 | A day of slight activity. In the evening we took in all lines and packed up and the battery moved out going about eight kilos to our new position in a large forest. We pitched our pups and put in our central on a tree.

SEPT. 24 | [*sic*]. Ran lines all day connecting P.C. 1st and 2d platoons and echelon. On the latter line Art and I worked all day utalizing about two kilos of german lines.

SEPT. 25 | Continued running lines today and now have everything in shape. Our longest line over 3 miles we put to our OP which is back of our position on a ridge to the left of Hatton-chatel. The place was shelled a bit while we were there. Vigenales is a heap of ruins at the foot of the ridge and is occupied by a few French troops and an American anti-aircraft battery. The boys have been hauling shells all day and we had thousands when we began a drum fire which lasted all night.

SEPT. 26 | We moved the central into a shack built by the Huns and have put bunks in an adjacent building where we are now very comfortably housed. Continuous fire all night. It being a demonstration to distract attention from our drive west of Verdun which is coming off in fine shape no doubt.[6] The situation is indeed fine.

General [Edmund] Allenby in Palestine has destroyed the Turkish army. In the Balkans we are extremely successful and here everything is our way.

SEPT.
27

With the 2 ration carts I went to Benay today and while out in the field digging potatoes whiz bang Fritz put one in front of us. Three in the field about us convinced us that he wasnt going to stand for it. I have watched from an O.P. our battery snipe at a few Huns but never had it happen to me. With little hesitation we took our spuds in hand and hightailed it, leaving poor old Benay to a nice bombardment. We came thru Pannes to see if we could get some supplies for the boys and then returned. We are going to Have the spuds fried for dinner tomorrow and I know they'll be good.

SEPT.
28

Our firing was average last night. We now have boco ammunition and have built a railroad track down to the first platoon to facilitate their transportation. The news on all fronts continues fine.

SEPT.
29

Mail came and I heard from all my friends. As usual we fire all night and rest during the day. Today Slaynan promoted a bill board and I filled it with prophaganda for our war orphans fund informing the boys as to who were the good scouts of the battery; how the voting stood as to whether our mascot should be a guy or girl etc. I also added some things to add interest such as a map of the Macedonian front with arrows and comments also remarks on the war by *famous* heroes of Bat. B. The board was called the Daily Latrine Squawk.

In the afternoon I went into the Echelon and collected 200 F. in about ten minutes everybody almost wants in on it so I think we'll be able to get two orphans.

SEPT.
30

Last night at midnight the Echelon line went on the blink and I was called to run it Netterfield volunteered to go along. We were pretty sure that a shell had broken it because they had been regularly going over our heads. Sure enough when we got up near the Echelon we came onto the place where our line was in pieces and the big shell hole was there (must have been an eight incher because she was a whopper[ )]. While fixing the break Fritz continued sending them over and we'd bite the earth between splices but it would have been no use because the boys bursted before the sound came to our ears. They were whiz bangers alright.

OCT. 1

Today we learn that 1st Lieut Hargett who was in command at the Echelon was hit by shell fragments in the legs and died on the way to the hospital. Later in the day "Coffin nail" Bradley was killed and Erickson and Linderman were sent to the hospital seriously wounded by the same shell.

In the evening we pulled stakes and moved in column to wood south of Nonsard. We are bound for the Verdun front we think because the Americans are driving there.

OCT. 1

[*sic*] This morning I left with reconnaisance detail and we rode about thirty kilos, when just out of Troyon we selected a place for the battery to put up tonight. There were ten of us in the detail and made good speed tho the road was over hilly country. Coming out of the plain to a great hill in line with Mount sec we could look over the territory which we are now battling over. We came over the old German & American trenches before Lacroix. This village is a heap of ruins but in it can still be seen many artistic creations. The cathedral was a very fine one and was peculiar to France in that it was built in the 20th century, a wash house was a little wonder built in renaissance style and there was an undamaged statue of high merit. On the journey we came by a vineyard and we stopped to get our helmet's full and then ate them on the way. The French soldiers we passed thought it a queer sight, officers and men riding along, eating from helmets. A queer sight was two Americans with two Hun prisoners riding in a Henry [Ford]. The prisoners were very young surely not over eighteen. After building a fire and getting a little food, Marsh and I went to Troyon to meet the battery. The night was the coldest of the year but Marsh and I kept moving and stuck it out. Still the battery didn't come.

OCT. 2

At dawn I spied a fire in a building and I made a bee line for it. I got warm and the cook gave me some bread and warm coffee. Soon the first of the brigade started through (149th leading) 151 followed and then 150th. We brought them to the position and then a few of us went over to the commissary in the next town where we got jam beans etc. After eating a big meal. We got in between the blankets and slept until 5 pm when we ate supper, fed horses and prepared to move. Our hike of less than 20 kilos took most of the night because of delays We stopped west of Rambluzen and the detail got a two walled shack to sleep in.

OCT. 3

Today Nitter, Stoltie and I took the little German cart back to _____ where we got the reel cart which had been lost on the hikes. While there we went to comissary and were lucky enough to get sugar, tapioca butter and hominy. This evening we made

IHS, Bretzman Collection

Gen. John J. Pershing, commander of the American Expeditionary Forces in Europe. Pershing was an inspiring leader who stressed rifle fire and open warfare. He successfully prevented the American forces from being placed under British or French command.

some candy. Ichabod, Marsh, Smith, Schwarz and I visited the next town where we heard a saxaphone sextett.[7] For breakfast we cooked hominy grits which were fine. Grazed horses in afternoon besides

OCT. 4

Usual grooming. Turned in early to tune of a fierce barrage from distant battlefront. At midnight we were awakened and began preparations for moving a breakfast was served and at [4:30?] we pulled out. We are going up to Verdun front. Where by sound of this cannonading which is still going, they must be having hell. Everybody is anxious to get into it. Along the way we were asked what outfit we were and when we said 42d their eyes poped out and the whole army along the way must have turned out to see us. At one town we saw a prison camp and one buck told us that they had captured 1900 yesterday and brought them in. Pershing's car was in another town but I didn't see him. One red cross officer along the way asked what div. we were and when told he said "Well here's where hospital trade picks up." which is more truth than poetry. Pulled into wood in afternoon.

OCT. 5

Had a good sleep last tonight in spite of the intense cold. I hope they issue us winter underwear soon. Today has been fine, plenty to eat for once. We groomed and in afternoon washed saddles. When going to water I saw a drove of about 100 burros. They were little fellows but carried a big load of ammunition. The barrage is still going as I close for tonight. I believe that we are held in readiness for a drive on any front so we may move up tomorrow if something happens. When we do go in something will happen because there is no parade resting when the Rainbows start the fireworks.[8]

7 | Meuse-Argonne

The greatest battle of the war for the American Expeditionary Forces opened on September 26 with an attack along the twenty-mile stretch of front between the Meuse River on the east and the Ardennes forest on the west. The Meuse ran north and turned to the northwest. The forest, half a dozen miles wide, reached north and tapered off into patches of woods and farmland interspersed with villages. The whole area had been held by the Germans since the beginning of the war, and the Germans were excellent fortifiers, so there was no easy place to initiate an attack.

A signal difficulty of the Meuse-Argonne sector was that it comprised an inverted triangle, its relative narrowness at the bottom spreading out fanlike to the north. When it reached the Meuse, the east-west distance, one end to the other, was sixty-five miles. Hence, troops had to be funneled in at the bottom in a constricted area with little room to maneuver and then spread out as the sector widened.

The goal of Gen. John J. Pershing's divisions was the city of Sedan, which lay at the top of the sector on the left side. Sedan was of symbolic importance to the French, for it was there in 1870 that the troops of Napoléon III surrendered during the Franco-Prussian War. The war was a military debacle that, among other humiliations, brought a German-imposed indemnity of four billion marks (one billion dollars) and loss of the provinces of Alsace and Lorraine.

Beyond the attraction of Sedan was the fact that just outside the city lay the double-tracked railroad that supplied German troops all the way to the English Channel. It was a vital line to German forces on the western front. If American divisions got anywhere near Sedan their artillery could sever the Germans' rail line.

In the mind of Marshal Ferdinand Foch there may have been a third purpose in giving the Americans the Meuse-Argonne. For months Foch tried to convince Pershing to bring American divisions into the French and British sectors of the front and place them if not under Anglo-French divisional command then under their corps and army control. Pershing, with the support of President Woodrow Wilson, refused. The Allied commander-in-chief may have thought that he would give the Americans a tough nut to crack. If they succeeded, that would be fine. If they failed, Pershing would have his comeuppance. The exhausted French and British divisions could not have defeated the Germans by themselves anyway, and the war would go over into 1919, by which time the Americans would have gained enough battlefield experience to carry the great conflict to a victorious conclusion.

For the first day or two of the Meuse-Argonne the U.S. divisions made excellent progress, until the German defenders brought in reinforcements. By October 1, with machine-gun emplacements everywhere and artillery fire enfilading the Americans from batteries in the Ardennes and on the heights of the Meuse River, the Germans had halted the Americans. As the conflict turned from one of movement into one of position, from the taking of kilometers each day to taking or retaking of a few hundred yards, Pershing called in his more experienced divisions, including the Forty-second.

OCT. 6

Fritz held a bombing party last night over the wood we occupy. He gave an exhibition of the fastest bombing I ever heard, the crashes for a time were as speedy as (sound of) machine gun bullets, however none of our outfit was touched.

This morning the brigade started forward and our path lay across the 4 yr. old lines of battle of French and Germans all of which have been recaptured by the Americans. Such a picture of desolation I never saw before. We came through a great forest and every tree in it had been shorn of life and those which still stood were naked, burnt and scarred. The ground itself resembled a choppy sea. Our engineers had to build bridges across it, for shell holes were so thick that one could not even walk between them. It seemed that every inch of ground had been struck by shell and often time the same hole had been struck repeatedly. We stopped for the night in this bleak forest and it was with the greatest difficulty that we found ground level enough on which to pitch a puptent. We watered our horses in shell holes and after feeding and grooming went to bed. The barrage has ceased but Fritz is shelling our back areas. The closest burst from our tent tonight however was 60 ft.

OCT. 7

This morning Fink, Dan, Marsh, Lt Vallingham and Captain and I saddled up and reported to the colonel where details of every battery assembled for instructions before reconuirtiring positions. The entire regiment located NE of Mont Facon. This town is a mass of ruins not a roof standing and practically every wall is leveled to the ground. A village we came through earlier in the day was an even worse example and its stone was being used for roads. It could scarcely be recognized as ever having been a habitation. Montfacon is on a high hill and from it can be seen a wonderful panorama the hills and val-

National Archives

Commanding officers of the 150th and 151st Field Artillery, Forty-second Division. Left to right: Col. George E. Leach and Col. Robert H. Tyndall, 1918.

leys are verdent with life now (it is newly occupied territory) and even the countless Boche bursts add to the picture an awful beauty. Even from our positions we can view the terrain for many miles.[1] At noon we ate mess at a 314 F.A. kitchen and to us it was a feast.[2] The enemy is shelling this area intensively and his harrasing fire is doing quite a bit of damage. One came within fifty yards of Col. Bob [Tyndall] even. In the afternoon Danny, Art, and I worked like blazes setting up central and running lines. Then at dusk we returned to mark the route for the battery. In the pitch dark I was riding ahead of a caisson and bringing it to the position when my horse stumbled in a shell hole and zip over his head I lunged into the mud, luckily so wasn't hurt the least bit. Art and Smithy and I finished the night by running the final line (to extra gun crew). The night was not especially pleasant with the H.E's froliking and gas alarms noisy. Our tent was showered with mud and fragment twice from HE's.[3]

OCT.
8

This morning Cliff woke us for mess and Grim and I got up amid a discussion of the German peace appeal to Wilson. The opinion was that the whiz bangs didn't sound like peace terms. I had just gotten my mess at the kitchen when I saw our tent. Cliff was stiffly sitting at the board screened by smoke and blown up. Smith and

Netterfield called for help but we were on our way with stretchers. Poor Art was dead mutilated all over, an arm clear off. Danny had a hole through his stomache but there are hopes that he will live, Cliff was seriously wounded about the legs and arms and Netterfield and Smithy were slightly wounded with fragments peppered over them. Netterfield did not go to the hospital. It is a great blow to me because tho we have lost men on every front these fellows are my best pals and I have worked with them especially Art ever since I joined the battery. The Chaplain came over and Art was buried with a simple ceremony. We are experiencing the fiercest cannonading in our service. Casualties every few minutes somewhere in the vicinity. I went over to the trench in which we had our central and got the switch board which was about the only thing left. A fragment had gone through it and destroyed the bell but otherwise it was good. While getting it a shell burst near me and I ducked in the trench and was hit a jolt in the small of the back but it was only a chunk of mud thrown up by the H.E. We now have all communications operating O.K.

OCT.
9

Last night we certainly returned Fritz's compliments with interest. We fired (harassing fire) all night and our entire side of the line did likewise so that at times it reached an intense drum fire. We are still giving it to them this morning.

This afternoon we advance. Going through Montfacon again to our next position near Exermont. The battery was firing a half hour after arriving. We are dosing Fritz with H.E.'s and kept it up all night. He in turn put over some close ones. Got a paper today and the news is great. Kaiser Bill sure is out of luck.

OCT.
10

We are giving Fritz all kinds of hell and I don't wonder that he is after peace.

I received two letters from the folks today.

Tonight as I was going to my bunk after scouting up some ammunition detail a shell exploded nearby and I got a good dose of sneezing gas. I sneezed and watered at the eyes and coughed but no harm resulted and I am now feeling good.

OCT.
11

A day of steady firing. This evening I went in to the Echelon to settle up for our second orphan and when I reached there I found that sudden orders called for the firing battery to be brought back to the Echelon in preparation for another move, so I hurried back. At the position we packed up and waited for the teams and wagons to come.

Paul and I went in search of a little warmth about midnight and found it in a 1st aid station where there were many wounded being treated Soon the horses came and the column moved by morning we reached the Echelon.

OCT.
———
12

After sleeping three hours we rose ate breakfast (rather the bat did. I felt sick indigestion etc and didnt want anything) and moved out with the tel detail. I rode ahead of the column with Lt Bennet and as usual marked the way. As we were going along two shells hit within ten yards of the road at this time half of our column was held near a provision dump by a ditched truck and I went back to find out the trouble just after I had found out the delay and had started back a big whiz banger landed right in the center of the dump. I was making speed by that time and a truck in front of me threw on the juice with such a jerk that a loaf of bread fell out of the back so I hopped off my chaveaux and grabbed it.

In the village of [Sherwood did not identify the village] we were held up quite a while due to the difficulty of getting up a big hill beyond it After we had climbed the hill ourselves, we found that half the battery had been delayed and Lt. Bennet sent me back to take charge of it to bring it up. I found it a couple of miles back and brought it up but I must say that it was a great relief when I got the whole column into the field with the rest of the outfit.

After messing the firing battery moved out with the detail in front walking (the roads were so bad that we left our horses.) It was already pitch dark and the conjested condition of the road made our progress slow. Especially at a certain town we were held up for a long time. I went ahead and found how the route was blocked at the crossroads and I went to work helping the lone M.P. out. He didn't seem to be able to get the French to move so I tried my hand at ordering them to pull up in certain places to free the road and finally succeeded in getting things going. The capt. and I walked ahead clearing the road as we went. One truck in particular had the road blocked waiting to unload ammunition and the driver was obstinate, but in my best general voice I ordered him up so my artillery could pass and it being dark the driver couldn't tell me from Pershing and he moved on the jump. at a cross roads we found that three wagons had been lost so the capt sent me back to get them through the traffic and bring them up. When I located them I found them in charge of Lt Smith and 1st sgt. patiently waiting behind a truck and fourgon wagon which were a stradle the road. It made me so mad I wanted to fight and it didn't take me long to get the truck to one side and the fourgon started up the hill, however the horses couldn't pull it so I got one of our extra teams and hitched on. It was then easy sailing and by the aid of markers the bat had left we were able soon to rejoin the battery. Our guns pulled into position and we spent the early morning in setting up communications.

OCT. 13

We have begun firing and have been supplied with a large amount of ammunition. We moved central to a building in the town (Exermont) only a few yards from the first gun. This town is not so badly shot owing to the fact that since 1914 the Americans are the only troops who have fought the Germans for it. The Huns are putting a few over at us and have hit the town today as well as placing several shells on the ridge ahead of us. During the night several shells exploded just in rear of the battery.

OCT. 14

At 8:30 a.m. the Rainbows went over the top. The artillery put up a fearful barrage for several hours, we used OA shells and Ial [Lal] fuses which makes the most powerful explosive to infantry we have its destructive area having a radius of 200 meters.

At noon Slim of the Alabama doughboys came back wounded in the hand (third time) and he said "Oh boy you all doan know how powerful that barrage of youalls is." Slim sang our praises saying how good it felt to have us paving the way for them. He said the slaughter among the Huns was terrible, however our ambulances are full also. Slim said that the doughs were suffering heavy casualties but were gaining their objectives and were sticking a lot of Huns.

Every one laughs at the peace outlook altho Germany has accepted Wilson's terms. With all this battling it is hard to think of a quick conclusion of the slaughter.

A correspondent came by this morning and took Nitz and my picture with some German armor we had found.

OCT. 15

It is now 5:30 a.m. and the roads are resounding with the sound of tanks which are rumbling up through the town. Two tank men came in the house central and we gave them a bunk. Two engineers are also sleeping in the same room with us.

This morning we attacked doughs preceded by tanks and getting the Boche by surprise we advanced 4 kilos. In Belgium the allies are driving and in the rest of France we are pushing the Huns back. Wilson is right in accepting nothing but unconditional surrender from the central powers. Turkey and Austria will comply toot sweet and then the Huns can't hold out long.

Our losses are heavy, a good many gassed but at that our gas is more deadly than their's.

OCT. 16

Div. captured a village today. The Huns counterattacked but after they gained two kilos we put over a barrage on them and cut them to pieces and our doughs gained additional ground. Our food is better—we eat in the signal corps line and today the

boys promoted some flour and we had all the pancakes we could eat. It is
a little more quiet than usual tonight but will no doubt pick up later.[4]

OCT. 17   This morning I set out with Major, capt, and Fink to hill which
we are to make our OP. This hill 316 is the highest on this terrain and is excellent for observing purposes. From it we can look
into the enemies position and detect his movements for miles. It
is right back of the 1st line and the reserve infantry is behind and on it.
The rear side of this hill is certainly thickly populated.[5] American doughboys have dug fox holes all over the rear side and in them they sleep. The
hill is about five kilos down the valley from Exermont, so running a telephone line to it was almost a day's job.

OCT. 18   A year ago we sailed at that time I predicted that a spring drive
by Allies would end the war before winter. It may come true in
spite of the fact that at that time we did not count Russia out of
it. The OP line went on the bum and I went out on it. When
working near posit of E bat. a duel was held above my head by one of the
Lafayette planes and a Boche.[6] The former gained the advantage of position and peppered the latter with bullets and he came hurtling to the
ground managing however to make a good landing, but while running on
his wheels the plane turned turtle and lay there. It was within 40 yds of me
and I was there in a jiffy (about first). The two occupants accepted capture.
They both crawled from under the machine the pilot only being wounded
through the breast. I got the observers cap. I must admit that the two were
fine looking young men, but one of them made me sore by asking in a
meek voice "sprechen sie Deutsche"? The victor swooped in circles about
us verifying his victory and then went away. It was the allies day because
three more Boche came down in quick succession.

OCT. 19   I was out early this morning and ran the tel line to O.P. getting
up on the hill at 10 am. with everything OK. I telephoned back
to the captain telling him that visibility was fair that I could pick
up our targets with my glasses and he sent up the observers.
Soon observers from every battery in the regiment were upon the hill
nearby were observers from dousins of outfits. The Boche knowing that we
would choose such a fine point has been trying to run us off and at times
one could not talk because of the schreeching and bursts of the projectales
which he hurled at us. G Washington once said that the whiz of bullets
were music to his ear but I'll bet he wouldn't think the scream of H.E. very
fine music, however Americans are all alike I guess for every time one
comes close to getting us we laugh and crack jokes about it nearly having

our numbers. Our batteries blew up several OP's and made the roads in Hunland deathtraps. We could see the Boche clearly with our binaculers. One scene which interested me was a small party (three) of Huns, who were coming toward our lines on some mission and were carrying a white flag with a red cross perhaps they were a machine gun squad playing a dirty trick but no one fired on them at any rate.

OCT.
20

Rain again today. The mud is very bad and I am afraid will delay our impending offensive. I am sure that we will launch an irresistabl drive toot de sweet for we have boco artillery and all of us have a vast amount of ammunition. They have given the Yanks the worst sector of the battle line and the Huns are opposing us with a large number of his best troops but we are going to get him right this time and I only hope we are not relieved before that time.

OCT.
21

I went to MD yesterday and he put iodine on my sore legs with result that today they are all blistered. I sent home my Xmas box containing the aviator's cap, a bit of propaganda etc. It is quite a sight to see an areoplane drop propaganda. It looks something like snow, with light playing on it, as it descends.

OCT.
22

[−] was out today and we actually got some clean under clothes and sox and an overcoat. Last night as per usual the Huns put some over between us and the church.

OCT.
23

At OP today. Battery tore up a wood occupied by Huns. Tonight we put over 100 gas shells.

OCT.
24

I am made corporal again.[7] The fighting is more bitter than ever but not a day passes but that the 1st army gains some ground.

OCT.
25

We are going to leave Exermont tomorrow. It is tough in a way because these old battered Hdq and cellars have made us cosy comparatively and the tanks and sig corps have kept us from starving.

OCT. 26 Pulled stakes today and at noon with the detail and Hun cart I set forth to the new position near Sommerance which the Capt. showed me on the map. At Fleyville I saw a kitchen which was serving doughnuts and since my only acquaintince with such things for a year has been through reading about them in the Stars and Stripes I stopped and bummed two fine ones. The roads are being heavily shelled. We lost some horses and had three drivers wounded. Our position is the most forward one we have yet taken. We have dug our foxholes in a big ditch.

OCT. 27 The Huns put over some gas tonight and shelled us. Our causualties for the night are five. Jimmie was one of them but he isn't serious.

OCT. 28 It is tough to stay here quiet while Fritz is dosing us with gas and shells but wait.[8]

OCT. 29 Went up to OP today while battery fired its first shots in this position. We are careful because we dont want Fritz to know where we are; but his areoplanes have found out any way. I was surprised to see from OP how close to Hun lines we are—about kilo and half.

OCT. 30 Last night he gave us hell and I don't see how any of us are alive to tell it. Shells exploded on every side and showered us with fragments and dirt. Outward line was knocked out and Grim and I repaired it during the inferno. I thot Id never see home and mother again but we came out OK. Jack Skull went to hospital with Shell Shock.

OCT. 31 Halloween night a year ago we pulled into the harbor of St Nazair so we are now entitled to wear two gold service stripes on our left sleeve. One gas casualty this eve. The 75 battery next to us had a funeral today, one of boys killed. At times I go over to the town to take care of my horse. Today after the 82d div had left there I found me a new pair of shoes I needed badly. The Huns shell the town at irregular intervals.[9]

NOV. 1 I shall never forget this day. At 3 o'cloc our barrage started and I believe that there has never been such a great artillery demonstration in the world's history. Lieut Bennet commanded load and the deafening roar broke forth not only from our guns but from thousands for it had been so wonderfully well timed that the fury was loosed on the dot. Our position is so far forward that battalion of machine guns operated behind us and their cracking was so monotonous and intense that actually at times they seemed to drown out the noise of our powerful howitzers. The good old 75s too were everywhere spitting out their destruction. Tongues of flames lept from the mouths of such numberless guns that the heavens were lighted as by electricity. For a time Fritz bombarded us but his bursts could hardly be distinguished in the turmoil.[10]

The doughs went over at 5:20 being met with a Hun barrage but they braved it and went forward until this evening they have exceeded all hopes and are still going. I'll tell you, one must have a prayer for those who have fallen and those who are suffering. In sommerance our aid stations are crowded with the brave lads who have lost limbs or jaws or other organs yet they do not even groan, simply smoke their cigaretts and stay silent. All Hun prisoners and there are many are made to carry back from the front the stretchers laden with our boys. Then they are herded together and sent to the cages while the wounded are sent to the base Hospitals in ambulances. The German wounded are taken care of the same as our own though we hate them. However one cannot but feel sorry for the mere children we have taken, poor fellows who still have kiddish ways and "know not what they do" and couldn't help it if they did.

Things have somewhat calmed down as far as we are concerned, some of our artillery is moving up the 17th moved up this morning.[11] We are prepared to go but are doing slow fire (maximum elevation [−] charge). Turkey has surrendered, Austria Hungary has capitulated, and I believe this blow will go a long way to bringing the Huns to their knees.

Today a bird flew near our battery during the chaos. It seemed stunned and no wonder when man has so upset the order of life. What a blessing will it be when mother nature has the running of the universe to herself again. Took up all lines today so tonight I stood up four hours on phone at P.C. Got letters from home gee but theyre a godsend. I did feel a little crabby with my injured legs and the boco cooties etc but the letters just put all jake again. A remarkable feature of the offensive was that the Rainbows kept going after reaching all their objectives. They were supposed to pause and allow the Marines to pass but no, they didn't want anyone to get ahead of them.

NOV. 2 The fighting on our left flank was intense last night and this morning the Huns attempting to outflank us but we nipped their scheme in the bud and sent them homeward. Prisoners say the war has never seen such terrible destruction as that caused

Members of the 150th Field Artillery billeted in the church for twenty-four hours rest, Bar, Ardennes, France, November 5, 1918. Troops were often billeted in houses or other structures in towns and villages.

by American artillery. We went on batallion reconnaisence detail today picking advanced posit past St Juven but didnt occupy them on account of brigade order to sit tight until further orders. It is raining tonight and leaking thru our hole in the bunk so I will have stop and try to fix it up.

NOV. 3   Doughs are chasing the Huns; who run like rabbits. In afternoon our battalion left Sommerance and travelled through the night at the snail like pace always experienced after a drive. In fact it was the worst night I have spent on the road with exception of Masidres-Seicheprey road at San-Mihil drive. It rained and we moved so seldom that we kept up our spirits by talking of what we'd eat when we got home. Came to Buzancy town proper is south one kilo.

NOV. 4   Our billet here is fine. I am sleeping on a bed with mattress the Huns left and we have a stove in the room which *is* luxury this kind of rainy weather. It seems that we are to be motorized. Lt Bennet asked me if I had had experience with motors and trucks. I said I had never driven a truck or Ford since I started driving ten years ago but I could do it. Bombers visited us again last night dropping about two hundred near here the boys say they must shove the bombs out via open endgate the way they fall.

NOV. 5 | A four-star car passed thru today, probably Black Jack [General Pershing]. Cleaned up my pistol and despite the inches of mud he held got him shining again.

NOV. 6 | We were prepared to move today but got orders to remain. The Y man brought us a few supplies today. He is a good scout but the organiz is simply too small for its great job. Got second class mail too. In eve we met Art and went to his and Flems room down the street and read Linton Citzs [*Linton Citizen*] (until bed).

NOV. 7 | Several truckloads of French civilians have passed through here going into the interior today. Austrian capitulation official as is Kaiser's abdication said to be. End can't be so far off. Had bath washed clothes and in eve visited Slayman who provided a feast of doughnuts + coco.

Encampment with soldiers and pup tents. The man in the foreground may be Col. Robert H. Tyndall.

IHS, Robert H. Tyndall Collection

NOV. 8

Had my legs bandaged up (coming fine). Washed saddle and wrote some letters. 42d div had honor to capt. Sedan.[12]

NOV. 9

We are now standing formations and will prob. fight a war of inspections. Terms have been given to the Huns and they are given to Mon 11 ocloc to accept or reject so we will soon know whether we stay the winter thru or not.

NOV. 10

After the usual day of various roumers we hiked forward to a field north of Harricourt where we pitched pup tents and turned in. Rather heavy firing tonight.

NOV. 11

We all cheered when we heard the news of course but we are more quiet in our happiness. everybody is singing to himself. At 11 the firing ceased the calm seemed queer but of course everybody is happy. We found a signal lights dump and tonight the skys are lighted with rockets and flares.[13]

8 | Germany

(NOVEMBER–DECEMBER 1918)

After the armistice Ferdinand Foch and the Allied leaders in Paris assigned zones of occupation along the Rhine River, and the Americans received an area that centered on the city of Koblenz. The commander-in-chief of the American Expeditionary Forces (AEF) gave his best divisions, including the Forty-second, the honor of occupying this zone, and it was their duty and privilege to march into Germany. For the infantry the task of transportation proved rigorous, for the terrain was up and down. Day after day the regiments hiked along the roads.

An attraction of Germany was the sight of picturesque places nestled—that was the word—along hills or in deep valleys next to brooks or rivers, all without damage from artillery fire. Germany had been far enough behind the lines to escape the terrible damage wreaked upon northern France. Another attraction was that unlike France the German villages were orderly and clean, no manure piles outside houses.

Troops discovered friendly behavior by the natives, villagers, and townspeople alike. Some of this was due to tiredness with the war. More was a result of the generosity of American soldiers whose commissaries were full of food and other items scarce in Germany; the troops shared their rations and made friends. Many of the men spoke German, and that made Germans and Germany more attractive.

NOV. 12

Sitting around the camp fire before the pup tent writing this tonight. We have spent the day in grooming horses and in washing harness—irony of war + peace. All day the boys have been sending up rockets and roman candles. The late papers we got tell of the Kaisers abdication. Paid. all boys shooting craps.

NOV. 13

Received mail, wrote letters.

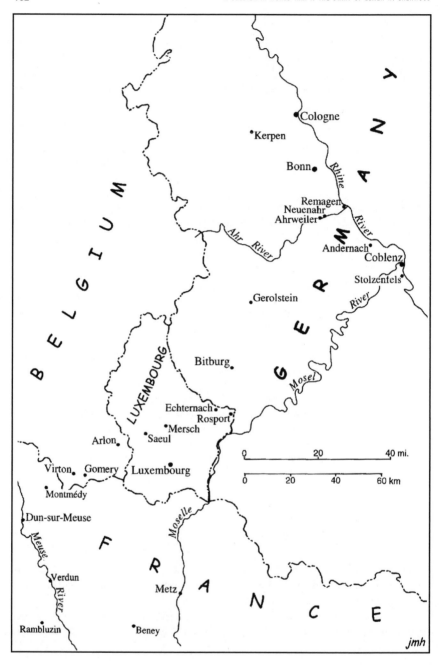

NOV. 14

In Imecourt before the big fireplace of some French family, which will perhaps return soon to reclaim it. The French fireplaces are smoky and fact is I would not call any of their arrangements comforts of home. They do not know really what living is. Nevertheless we are spending some pleasant hours before the fire gassing. Already we are reminiscing about events of our army careers really I pity the folks at home.

NOV. 15

The boys played poker in spare time which isnt boco. Received 75 new horses today and will get 20 men tomorrow so it seems certain as the Chaplain says that we are Germany bound. Wherever our destination is I hope we don't linger here long. This waiting is exasperating since the war is won.

NOV. 16

Cold windy day spent at horse lines. The ____ officers demand grooming about 8 hrs a day and even had us to wash pieces and wagons today. Moved 4:30 over hilly country arriving at _____ in the evening at 9:00 pm—16 kilos—biting wind walked to keep warm and talked to Ich.

NOV. 17

Slept on ground in field last night when we built a bonfire to keep warm. The only trouble with our fires made of Hun ammunition baskets is that sometimes something explodes. We have had four men sent to hospital by such accidents. [illegible] at 1 arriving at Ansermont at 8 pm via Dun where we crossed Meuse river.

NOV. 18

On picket line all day caring for horses. These ____ officers must think that they will have us under their power for a few months and they want to exercise it while they can. Because some of the boys were late for reveille the capt made us move from our billets to the open field (it snowed some today first time this winter). So tonight I am again writing by the light of the bonfire. We're called heroes at home but are treated as dogs here.

We were each issued a leather "jerkin" (vest) Today it is fine and warm. Mullholand acquired a Deutchhund on the hike yesterday. He is as ugly as the Clown Prince.

Ich, Land, Asher and I are about the fire, and the talk drifted to girls + slackers. Asher told of his girl having to marry at home a slacker. I said did you love her? "Did I" he said in a lower tone. "I was engaged to her." What a tragidy in his life. One sometimes does not know what is in his closest comrade's heart.

Visited Nig at his billet earlier in the evening but it was warm in the room and my cooties being livened up, demanded that I move. Thank goodness that we get a bath tomorrow. Mail today I got one from dad, Mom, Amelia + Louise.

NOV. 19 Took a bath today (2 minutes). In the evening we found some Deutsch flour and made pancakes but they didn't amount to much because they were doughy in the center. Saw a Herald today.[1] Telling of the composition of the third army—army of occupation. It includes 1 2 3 4 5 26, 32, 42 82 and 90th divs. The paper said that 1, 2 and 42 were most famous and gave us the best boost of the three.

NOV. 20 Arose at 5:30 groomed, fed, provisioned and moved out being on the road all day with average speed only. Passed thru Lecself, Ire le Sec, and arriving at Montmedy just as the populace were loudly proclaiming the arrival of Poncair [Raymond Poincaré] and his retinue. I got a good view of the president of the republic. He is of very sallow complection being no doubt worn out by the responsibilities which are his. His wife, generals and officials were there This is the first time we have seen civilians other than refugees and stragglers for many weeks so the undamaged city decorated with flags was a welcome and pleasant sight. On the outskirts of this town were several ordnance shops with many German cannon.

NOV. 21 Slept last night in a barracks of a Hun prison camp. Left town this morning at end of brigade column. We crossed the Franco Belgian frontier this afternoon and from appearances Belgium is a more prosperous land in peace than France. Some towns have been burned as punishment and civilians tell us of many crimes of the Boche. One woman said she was thrown out of her house naked and with her half year old baby.[2] Everybody was at the point of a bayonet asked to choose between Germany + Belgium. Virton is a fine city. The inhabitants were out to greet us and I don't see where all the flags come from. The home made American flags are everywhere and are amusing being made of every material imaginable. One I saw had a blue white dotted calico cloth for the field of the flag. The greatest difficulty seemed to be the number of stars and they vary greatly. Pulled into village of Gomery in the evening and put our picket line and pitched pups in a field nearby.

NOV. 22 Left Gomery at 10 am with billeting detail and we came along at a good pace. Passed thru Arlon. It has a fine cathedral. Everywhere now the towns have arches and evergreen trees are put along the roadside Out of Arlon we took the wrong road and rode into Luxumburg. They have the Belgian and allied flags displayed there as everywhere now. We turned back and took a short cut to the town where we are assigned Girsch. Here we were at ease a few hours before the battery came and we went to a house where the family was just sitting down to dinner, but nothing would do but that we should sit down to a meal of potatoes, flap jacks and (coffee made of wheat). We asked the price after we had finished and she said in German which is the language prevailing here on the Luxumburg border tho French + Belgian are common perhaps the latter more so.[3] "We are all one family now that peace is here and I will be a mother to you all." The potatoes came from the U.S. and given free she said [page corner torn] old man showed us his empty [—] and said that the Huns had robbed the whole country. This town, village rather, is decorated as for a Christmas festival evergreens flags colored paper etc.

We were billeted with a family, who treated us fine. The man making a fire. We are able to buy apples at 1/2 F or 10¢ apiece. The people are splendid nevertheless and are not trying to profiteer.

NOV. 23 Moved out at 7 a.m. with detail, crossing Luxumburg border within a few minutes noticing a lack of flags. We picked our position at Saeul having some trouble with billeting from the pro Germans but we had to occupy their lofts just the same. We occupied the first of our billets where the citizens had protested and it was not long before they thawed, and became very friendly. One of the boys got some white flour and sugar and soon the Frau had made us some splendid "panacooken," which seemed to melt in our mouth. She seemed to take a liking to me and took delight in handing me the hot plates full and making me carry them in my hands (howling) into the dining room My influence also seems to be based on two stripes since they think an "unteroffiser" is *something* also I am the only one in the bunch who sprechens any Deutsch at all. I know about ten words which I employ on all occasions and can ask for "schnapps" for the boys one stranger a passing truck driver had me request some for him and said, "you speak splendid German don't you and I replied Yes very fluently.["]

The Frau cooked a good supper for us charging 45F. Everything is higher here than any place we have been (a chicken 25F). Fine sleep in the hay mow.

NOV. 24 Sonntag—The old man brought a light out as we were getting up this morning and invited us to dress by the fire. We took care of the horses and came back to the warm room where I am writing this.

For some unaccountable reason the officers permitted us three hours off today and the band gave a concert in the public place this being the only time I have heard the band play in months.

We have found now that the inhabitants were glad for us to come into the country. The Germans took all they could get their hands on when they left, including potatoes. They became curious when one American a scout came then six or seven soldiers listing billets and the people then were glad because they knew others would come and they did infantry companies first who stopped followed by artillery, which went on. They say that some of the boys went on and ran across some Boche in a school house. They shot one American, and when the smoke cleared away the Boche were finis.[4]

Tonight we had a chicken supper at very reasonable price, first chicken I had had since Guer a year ago I believe and she made wonderful coffee. I looked over the Luxumburg paper and it is full of the story of American + French occupation and tells of the presence of [John J.] Pershing and Foch.

NOV. 25 This morning Sgt Bowers Rorick, Campell and I were given 12 hr passes to Luxumburg and were to leave on regt. truck at 9:[5] After waiting the hour we were told the truck couldnt go because of lack of gas, so I caught a truck and went to Mersch, a good sized town nine kilos east of Saeul. Spent the morning with some other fellows of batallion trying to get a truck to Lux. but was unsuccessful, so we looked over Mersch, getting a good meal for 7 marks. The only cheap thing in town was a hircut for half a franc; candy was terribly high about $5 a pound.

In the center of town was a huge arch which said "Honor to our liberators." The police here were dressed like major generals. In a small shop I talked to a Luxumbourger who had lived in St. Louis, she had returned just a month before war broke out and had to stay. She told me that the standing army of Luxumbourg numbered 400. Returned in eve via truck and hit the straw tired and slightly disappointed that I hadn't reached my destination; but I may get there yet.

NOV. 26 Under a very stringent schedule now we have practically no time to ourselves. It is hard to get a minute to shave in. Grooming the hair off the chevaux and squads right share equally.

In evening five of us had a meal at the house where we stay in the loft. The old lady and gent are kind and give us the use of their front room at all times. The meals of these people are perhaps not so dainty as the French but there is more substance. They are big eaters, so are we.

NOV. 27 Usual day of drilling and caring for horses. It rained all day but in spite of it we were kept at the picket line all day.

Halliburton got some flour today so tonight we are taking it to an old woman where we will have waffles (nicht gute).

Battery took a bath today. Our old lady called me back today to kitchen where she and the old man performed gymnastics demonstrating to me that one of the soldiers had cooties the scratching being circumstantial evidence I asked how many they had seen and they said one, so I seriously promised to investigate and take measures, of course. We all have them. On guard tonight.

NOV. 28 Thanksgiving day—muddy but not so cold as the day is at home generally. On guard so after posting my relief I came up to our billet room and wrote letters.

At the kitchen we had a fine dinner—roast beef dressing, potatoes, gravy and apple pie. I had plenty but not enough to get the belly ache, so when invited to eat panacooken with the Frau and Mann and Halli I didn't refuse (2 ocloc) Thereby hangs the tale of my undoing, for we cut the stack of cakes in four parts and it seemed to be the hard and fast rule that when one took his part each of us should also they were to be eaten from the hands (no tools allowed) Well I stuck out to the last leaving only a little piece which I left not being able to get it down. The Frau insisted that it wasn't good manners in vain. I felt rather dizzy and retired to my bunk full and the old thanksgiving ache.

NOV. 29 It rained most of the day while we washed saddles. In the afternoon there was a band concert and some of us who had harness finished attended. The band is rather good now. The feature which the civilians seemed to enjoy most was the slide trombone.

Today the old man's brother in law came over and we were surprised to find that he talked excellent United States having been over in God's country eighteen years ago. He said that this was the first time he has spoken our tongue since that. Tonight promoting detail did well.

NOV. 30 Usual day with addition of a band concert. Shook made doughnuts and pom de terre and we had a fine meal. I took the old woman some she liked the former saying they were made in Deutschland but didn't like the latter style.

The Luxumburg flag is displayed now Red, white and blue horizontal stripes.

DEC. 1 Left Saeul this morning at 8. I bade the old folks good bye and got their address: Euggen Lebdntopon a Saeul. They seemed sorry to see us go and the Frau kept telling me that I wouldn't have any stove in Deutschland like I had had here.

Went ahead with reconnaisance detail going thru Mersch. Then we got among the hills making a mistake in roads and finally getting back on the track after following a path where we came to our destination, Bluscheid. We picked out billets and awaited the battery. After we had become settled I went over to the hay loft (billet) to sleep because I didnt feel well only to be routed out for a mission but when I returned slept like log.

DEC. 2 We have just arrived at Rosport and am writing this in Cafe du Cömmerce (the name proves that French is still familiar here) across the street is Hotel zur Post (Deutsch).

The town is in a deep valley with high hills surrounding it, hills as large as the Appalacians.

Our journey all day has been through a very picturesque country a greater part of it through a great valley. One town was especially picturesque sitting among the hills the streets being at different altitudes. Some houses were built on cliffs so steep in appearance as to seem inaccessable. Steep cliffs of hard rock surmounted with pines made beautiful pictures. On the latter part of the hike we had gradually been going higher when suddenly we came to the crest and looked down upon this deep valley Looking down we saw spires and housetops of several villages snuggled in different parts of the valley. Some of the best houses I have seen since coming across are here. The canal which is close by marks the boundary between Germany and Luxumburg.[6]

DEC. 3 Left Rosport at 9 reconnaissance detail and after we had travelled a few kilos a motor cycle rider came up and told us that the orders were to rejoin the column, so we returned and fell in behind the colonel.

The hike was thru beautiful but hilly country at 10:00 we crossed the bridge from Echternach to Echternach Brach. There was not such a difference in the houses but the people of course look very Boschish, especially the boys with the soldier dunce caps.

The people are very servile in attitude seem scared. One man asked if the Americans had enough leather and when told that we had he said "Then you won't take the leather off the seat of my pheaton?["] The people look at us in dumb and scared way with one exception a little fellow who had more spirit than the entire german army was hurling rocks at us with all his might and his face wore a militant and defiant look. He was about five years of age. One woman saw us coming and in a flash drug in her daughter (about 13) and slammed the door. They need not fear that the Americans will act as barbaric as their own soldiers.

I am writing this tonight in the living room of a German family. Mutter is darning socks in a chair across from me. Frauline is mending one by my

Bird's-eye view from Landskrone mountain peak. The Heppengen and Appolinaris water plant is in the foreground, and the city of Ahrweiler (Bad Neuenahr-Ahrweiler), Germany, is in the distance, December 1918.

side on the same bench and the boy (21) a fine looking chap is reading a book at the other end of the table. He has only last week exchanged his Hun uniform for civilian clothing. He was in the artillery but is very anxious not to offend us now. The old man is sitting by the side of the window. He just got through filling his pipe with P.A. and demonstrating to me how to light the pipe in the best way as he calls it.[7] He has a steel instrument which fits on the hand and he strikes the piece of flint a blow and the resultant spark lights the piece of punk which he holds on top of the flint.

These people are extremely hospitable mainly perhaps because they want to please us so that we wont treat them mean. (Imagine Americans doing that) We built a fire in back yard and made pan cakes. The old man hovered about bringing wood etc in a submissive way. We gave the family a bunch tho they tried to refuse (they are not at all beggars) and they had quite a time discussing the merits of soldier cooking and they really were good.

Symmetrical plowing and farming of hill sides.

We have had this evening a discussion about the table concerning the war and other subjects. Our young college German wanted to know what we are going to do with the Rhine territory we are occupying. We tell him that America wants no territory and we think will return it when the peace is signed. I discussed school Ceaser's Latin etc with the fellow as best I could since he can speak French. Joe came in and facilitated discussion with his fluent German. The people did suffer some for lack of food. Two families in twelve have before the war left for America and these people tell us of people in Kansas and Minnesota etc.

The old man said that we had come under peculiar circumstances but that they were surprised at our kind treatment of them. He said we could sing "Die Wacht am Rhine["] with a meaning of its own.

DEC. 4

Came ahead a seven to where the people take their defeat with the same good grace. I talked to two machine gunners who still wore their army pants and boots, because of the high cost of clothing here (500 marks a suit). One had been before us at Exermont and Chau Thierry and the other at St Quentine. They looked at the pictures in the Post and simply laughed when they came to picture of an Amer plane bringing down a Boche. They were much interested in my box stirreps.

I am writing this by lantern light in a hay loft of a man whose three brothers and a father in law are in Milwaukee.

For the fifth time since leaving the U.S. we had biscuits tonight at the kitchen.

DEC. 5

Today our line of march included Bitburg, here I was surprised to see German officers in uniform strutting about (but perhaps they have no other clothes to wear). There are some fine residences here and the headquarters of the third army is located in one large building with the officers occupying residences.

A German lieut Col was at Finks side when he bought a package of cigarretes and he remarked Americans must have plenty of money to buy such expensive things. Yes Fink replied. We have plenty of two things money and good soldiers.

A[t] mess this morning an ex-soldier said to us (he was looking on) If we had won the war we would have fought on until we had conquered the world. I am glad you ended the misery.

Another fellow however ran more true to form than any we have seen. He is the old Junker style Prussian. He said there would be another war in 50 yrs and Deutschland would make it on France. He said that Deutschland uber alles was the way things would and should stand.

Tonight we are in the house of a family with four Kinter and they are playing cards. I have looked through one of their school books and find it chuck full of Kaiser stuff.

DEC.
6

Marsh, Halliburton and I have just sat down to a white clothed table for supper. Die Fraulein has made a fire in the stove and brought in white coffee cups and I am sitting on a cushy seat all very homelike. The fact is these Germans are treating us better as a whole than almost anyone since we left America excepting the Belgians. Tonight they have put on their hand fancy work cloth and spruced up in general for us. When we came in the room we were confronted by big water color pictures of Bill and the Kaiserine. We laughed good naturedly and the girl acted as if she were covering it up.

The journey today was through the same rough and hilly country. We arrived in the town as the 17 F.A. 2 div was pulling through, this being the first time I had seen another division on this march. General [George C.] Gatley is quartered at the hotel here. He is a good looking fellow of about 50 yrs, and is commander of the best brigade of artillery in France (ahem)[.]

I have had a chance to learn the opinion of other Germans some of them being opposed to us in battle. The soldiers all say that they would have won the war had not America entered it, most of them however are glad that we came in and defeated the militarism of the Huns which offered them as well as the world no peace. The fact is, the German people are home loving and peace loving but their teaching for years had influenced them to believe Germany should rule the world and defeat was the only thing which could awaken them. Now the people say they would rather have us as guests than their own soldiers. We are cleaner and more polite they say.

We asked of one ex-soldier if he knew any of our divisions and he said that they had heard of the 42d or (and he gave the German name for Rainbow[)].They were told that we took no prisoners so they must not give up but fight to the end. He said they could tell American artillery because after four or five shots they hit the target.

Tonight we invited the German to eat with us and we learned that his son had been blinded in Italy. He showed us the boy's picture (an officer) and some souvenirs (booty no doubt) which he had sent home. He is now in a Berlin University studying law. I remarked that it was better now that the war had ended and he said that the end was a long way off. Germany was whipped and out of it he said, but England and France would fight over territory and though we wanted no territory we would no doubt take sides. These Deutsch sure have all of England's sins down pat.

Another fellow said Germany would be able to sell all her war supplies when Japan and the US got into it. The propaganda of the Huns has succeeded in some way.

DEC.
7

Geralstein. A featherbed? for once we were lucky enough to get one Hally and I, and we are retiring early to get the most out of it. We are in the house of a man who was in the Landsturm in service in Russia. He and his beautiful daughter are very hospitable.

Ichabod went to the hospital this morning. He has been sick (stomach and bowels[)] for a month and though I was sorry to see him go I know it was best.

DEC. 8

Kerpen. Tonight we are again in the midst of hospitable people. We have two beds here the Marshes Halli and I and this evening we brought flour and the fraueline made us some wonderful waffles.

I have been talking? to the old folks (groszmutter un father[)] and they say America helps Germany. They are like most of the Germans glad that we pitched in and ended it all for they say even if they had won they would have kept on fighting.

One German we talked with today had been in Michigan 18 years ago and could talk English. He called the Kaiser every kind of a _____ and said the officers would have been glad if the war had gone on forever for they had it soft while the peasants and common soldiers suffered. He said he would be glad if the U.S. would take over this country and run it in American fashion.

DEC. 9

We did not leave this village today and I understand that we are to remain here a day or two more. The people of this family certainly are treating us finely. Tonight we brought some more flour and the girls made us some more fine waffles. We also brought some coffee and the old lady was much surprised, since it was the first she had had since 1914, she showed me her coffee (parched wheat) The younger girl is a very hard worker she washed my clothes today and when I gave her five marks she wanted to give about four in change but of course I made her keep it.[8]

DEC. 10

On guard last night and today. The four of us brought our food from the kitchen and they prepared dinner for all of us the soldats and five Deutsch. They say they want us to stay here and live with them.

DEC. 11

Yesterday the first batallion held a review here with band, being on guard I was a spectator and enjoyed the sight very much. Tomorrow I hear there is to be a regimental parade.

It rained most of the day today, but we were out drilling and caring for horses just the same.

The old lady wanted to be especially nice to us today and made us waffles from her German flour and they were very good.

Today at a formation the captain read us an order telling us to keep a dignified mien and not to be either friendly or antagonistic toward the people. Our friendly relations are now beyond recall. They all hope U.S. will take over this land and we will stay with them.

In Germany as in other European lands morals are lax, for instance tonight a lady and daughter came in to visit and I said that among other things we had plenty of beautiful maidens in America. I said Halli that was my Frau and the lady blandly declared that He was not warm enough. which brought and uproarious laugh. Nothing is thought of sexual matters anyway.

DEC. 12 This morning on the picket line Revenau came for me and said I should report to Lieut. Paul at the school house. I went and found that I was to help check up battery equipment. All the boys brought their equipment to the school house. We made lists of it and then inspected the empty billets, to see that nothing was left in them. Then the boys were permitted to return to their billets. The idea of it all is to get rid of all extra equipment.

I am on guard tonight. After I had posted the first relief I came back to the house and sat around reading with the family and comrades. Some one proposed making candy. We had some sugar and I had a little can of coca which I had carried for a long time so we made fudge and it was fine. The family liked it as well as we did and goodness knows it was a great treat to us.

Of course Christine, who is three years old enjoyed it, for she doesnt know what candy is. She is a beautiful child, reminds me of Kate, and she has become very fond of us and always wants to play. I tell the folks that she should go to America with us, and they say if we will come back for her in a few years she will go. The old folks say they would go but for the gray hairs.

DEC. 13 On guard today. This morning I was initiated into the mysteries of threshing wheat with a flail. It was awkward at first, but I soon got the hang of it until father said I was good but of course he was kidding.

This afternoon Halli and I went up to the castle and climbed to the top of the tower. The castle, which is in ruins with a rugged wall and jutting towers, has been rebuilt in part with the stones from the ruins. A high tower has been built behind and looming above the modern residence which has also been constructed perhaps in the last 100 yrs. The old part dates from 900 A.D.

We obtained a fine view of the surrounding country which is beautiful at this season with its varied and subdued colors. The hills are symmetrical somewhat as in Lorraine and they are covered with thick forests. The more gradual slopes are of course cultivated and the plow has patterned the soil into many designs.

Catherina returned from Hillsborough with some things which seem to be secret. She told us about seeing an American darkey over there and

National Archives

Old wall and gates, dating from the middle ages, around at the south end of Ahrweiler (Bad Neuenahr-Ahrweiler), Germany, 1919. This city was in the Forty-second's zone of occupation in Germany.

Mutter was scared stiff at the description of the knife he wore on his belt. But we calmed her and told her they were bad men when it came to war but gentlemen toward civilians.

Christina baked a cake today and kept it under cover until tonight when she brought it in and we had a delightful repast.

DEC. 14
We rose early and along with the billeting detail left Kerpen at 8:00 the battery leaving two hours later. The four of us stopped at Bich's to say goodbye. Tears flowed freely even father cried and they made us promise again that we would write from America as well as from the town of our destination.

The trip was through the beautiful hills and at times we seemed to double on our tracks the roads were so crooked.

We spent the night in Arhweiler on a hard floor.

DEC. 15
Mail arrived last night and will be distributed after the hike today. The days journey was along the Ahr.

Spent the night in Rhden and were fortunate enough to get a good meal in the evening at 2 marks each which is a price very gratifying to our flat purses.

9 | Neuenahr

Neuenahr is a delightful town and when Elmer Sherwood's regiment established billets there they were seeing the best of provincial Germany. They remained until the Forty-second Division went back to the United States for demobilization.

The town is medieval in origin, crooked streets filled with narrow half-timbered houses interspersed with small churches, all largely untouched by later architecture. Shops cater to townspeople, farmers, and tourists. For the last, hotels are necessary, and Neuenahr is full of them. They are not, incidentally, for the rich members of German society but the *haute bourgeoisie* who save each year for their vacations of a few days, a singular splurge when they stay in a hotel and have their meals served to them.

Present-day American tourists, of a certain age, find a special attraction in that after taking a local train with its stiff-backed wooden seats through a winding line that in a half hour or so comes down to the main line along the Rhine River, the line that goes to Cologne, it is necessary to change at Remagen station, and looming on either side of the river are the huge masonry towers that until 1945 supported a railroad bridge. This bridge at Remagen was the span that retreating German forces in World War II only partly destroyed before an American infantry squad found the bridge, fought their way across, and in the few days before the bridge collapsed opened the way for the American army to cross the Rhine and enter the heart of Germany.

DEC. 16

Our journey today was through country as beautiful as I have ever seen. Our route was through the Ahr valley a pretty crystal stream filled with rapids. At times the road and stream were in deep gorges. The hills often displayed a rock surface and rose almost straight up.

Another wonderful thing about the land is that the hills are covered with vineyards. What a vast amount of energy the people have spent in terracing these great hills and in putting their rockey surface into cultivation.

National Archives

Bird's eye-view from the Landskrone, looking up the Ahr valley with Heppengen on the right and Neuenahr and Ahrweiler (Bad Neuenahr-Ahrweiler) in the distance. The Ahr valley, which is named for the Ahr River, a tributary of the Rhine, is noted for its mineral springs and red grapes.

Another display of their great toil is the railroad which runs through the valley. It is built among the hills and steps aside for none of them but is tunneled through solid rock in hundreds of places. Some of the great tunnels of Europe are here.[1]

Our destination Neuenahr is a very pleasing town, being a resort for the rich in summer, its mineral baths being the attraction (perhaps we can rid ourselves of some of our cooties)[.]

We have a room in the Villa Eden a beautiful building and our room which perhaps is a dining room is a fine one with electric lights and great windows looking out over the town.[2] We (detail) have six beds in it and a large writing table besides closets for our clothing and there is plenty of room.

DEC.
17
I am on guard again so have more spare time than usual which I am spending in writing letters.

Had a bath last night and sent my only suit of underclothes to the laundry today so I have to wear my overcoat to make up for the loss.

Played a game of billiards tonight and naturally was off. Did about as well as I could do the latest dances I presume.

DEC. 18

Spent the usual day on the line (picket) grooming and I also washed my saddle thoroly.

The kitchen has been moved to the basement of the hotel next door to us and we are using the dining rooms of the hotel. The noncoms have a separate room from the others. Personally I would rather have it all together. We are no better than the privates and have all endured the same things thru the war so are entitled to the same consideration.

Tonight we went down town and attended the movies, but they were German pictures and, hence no good so we didn't stay.

In a shop where I stopped to buy some raisins was a lady who spoke good English and we had a conversation. She said that the people were glad the Americans came for they liked us and were having no trouble with us. However the French and especially the British were treating the Germans roughly (for which I don't blame them) and the newspapers try to keep the feelings aroused.

DEC. 19

We have installed telephone communications and have put the central in our room so have to stand guard day and night. My relief tonight was from 9 to 12.

DEC. 20

Received some mail three letters and three magazines today. One of the boys found a can of pumpkin in one of the wagons so we had a woman make us a pie and found it delicious.

DEC. 21

A program was held at the YMCA tonight and the chaplaine announced that on authority of the colonel he could state that we were going home Jan. 10. which statement created a sensation.

DEC. 22

Picket line. At 2 p.m. Ingram and I went to church. It had been turned over to the regiment by the German people and the chaplain conducted the services. In his sermon he said that the failure of the doctrine Peace on earth, good will toward men was mans failure, not Gods.

DEC.

23

On the picket line again. Received a cablegram from Dad asking if I were O.K. It was sent Nov. 11th I think so no doubt my letters of that date have already reached home.

It rained all day and we had to drill, squads east in spite of it. however my time was spent in putting a telephone line in to Sgt Fultz's office.

This evening a non-coms meeting was held and Lieut Paul told us of the new program of drills which included four nights a week at school. Our time is to be completely occupied after Christmas week. Of course this isn't pleasing to me because I want to write as much as possible.

DEC.

24

It is 3 a.m. and I am watching the switchboard this Xmas eve morning. I looked out the window and see there is no snow on the ground.

The regimental band gave an entertaining program at the local theater tonight. After the show B Battery repaired to its hotel where beer and cigars were given out and more fun was indulged in.

DEC.

25

Thank goodness it snowed today and gave us the old Christmas atmosphere. Our dinner was fine: Christmas dinner Neuenahr Germany, Dec. 25, 1918. Bat. B. 150 F.A., Rainbow div. Prime Roast Beef (positively not chevaux) Brown sauce Baked onion dressing, Kaiser's own cold slaw. Cream Popickels Indiana cobbler Homemade cakes Bread Butter and jam Coffee milk and sugar Cigars and cigarettes music by bugler, "Your in the army now."

Entertainment at the YMCA was also good in the evening.

Last night and today I was on guard. Last night one of the picket line guards came up to me and told me that one of the horses had gotten loose. I asked him why he didn't go after it and he said, "It is too dark" Well I was as mad as a hornet at his spine less attitude and went out in a field and got the horse, which was peacefully grazing. But to my surprise I collected two more on coming in, after giving the guards hell I found that they were drafts which accounted for their lack of initiative.

DEC.

26

Reconnaissance detail went to position in sight of rhine and selected position for use in emergency. Ich and I played some billiards Ich winning 2 best out of 3.

DEC.

27

Halli and I bought a doll for Catherina at Kerpen and sent it. In evening Halli, Secrist and I ate supper at Claras a fine meal. Received three letters in the mail.

National Archives

A large white stone bathhouse built in 1899 and part of the Neuenahr Health Resort, used by Americans for a hospital and an infirmary, December 29, 1918. The town was visited yearly by thousands of patients.

DEC. 28 — Today my guard on switch board is 3 to 6 and have had rest of day off. Which time I have spent in reading and writing. I beat Ingram in a game of billiards for 50 points. which reminds me of a passage I read today in a Scribner's article entitled, "Americans as Frenchmen see them" by G. Rodrigues. "Against professional soldiers, against veterans trained in all the devices of the war, it has tested the strength of its young *volunteers* perhaps still somewhat inexperienced, but fighting for an ideal and not for a master."

DEC. 29 — Have begun writing my book Rainbow Hoosier. Have received so many requests from all the boys for copies of my diary that I believe this will be a success.

DEC. 30 — Took a bath at Kurhause. Tubs are built in floor—water is very hot and has a muddy look but is very refreshing.

DEC. 31

Usual day. In evening went to the movies and saw some punk films, no wonder the mfg. are so liberal as to give them away for our use.

JAN. 1

Stood muster. We had an excellent dinner roast beef, potatoes, and dressing. The Colonel came over to our mess hall and wished us a H.N.Y.?

JAN. 2

Spent most of day on picket line. In eve went to hotel Kurhause where we had some wine sherbert. Then went to Y where heard Burr McIntosh in a lecture and he read a poem of his own composition about our doughboys which was wonderful.

JAN. 3

Played in foot ball game today. We played a rough game and not being used to it I felt like _____ afterward. But just the same it was a joy to handle the old ball again.

JAN. 4

Inspection in morning. Halli and I climbed the highest hill in this vicinity from which we could see the Rhine.

JAN. 5

We were supposed to be paid today but there was nothing doing in that line. Bought a few trinkets to take home to the folks. Mail came with four letters and the Xmas box which contained real chocolate bars, a knitted helmet from grandma knife from Uncle Pete, fountain pen M.G. and watch fobs.

JAN. 6

Regimental parade today was a very impressive sight. I hope we do as well when we parade at home.

In evening I had a chance to put in some good licks on my book.

JAN. 7

Review by Maj Gen. [C. A. F.] Flagler and inspection of entire regiment.

JAN.

8

Paraded in honor of Ex President [Theodore] Roosevelt who died today. He was the greatest American and the soldiers feel his loss more than anyone because of his four A.E.F. sons and the fact that he wanted to be one of us himself.[3]

JAN.

7

Day on switch board night writing.

JAN.

8

Took care of Loco [?] today.

JAN.

9

Had a nice football game in the mud today. My only pair of trousers were caked with mud, as well as my exposed anatomy.

JAN.

10

Bat. went on road hike in morning.
     Played billiards in eve.

JAN.

11

Went down to H.Q. in evening and Cottie + I went to cafe where we talked over his illustrations for R.-H. Saxophone sextett gave a program tonight.

JAN.

12

Sent in mans. for R.-H. Read magazine in evening.

JAN.

13

Parade afternoon. Fisher came in this afternoon with an enlarged lip and a black eye. He had a fight over a horse blanket and though he got the worst of the combat he got the blanket. Entertainment by Band at Kurtheater.

JAN. 14 Another review this afternoon. Chaplin Nash gave interesting talk on causes of the war at non-coms school this evening.

Went to Ahrweiler today (Halli with me) and we visited commissary where we bought goods for the battery. Got choc. cigarettes and velvet.

JAN. 15 Drilled all day taking about equal time on posit aiming drill, calisthenics battery marching, standing gun drill. Am writing this in the Kur Theater where the 151 band is going to give a concert.

JAN. 16 Ichabod and I had our pictures taken. Stood an inspection.[4]

JAN. 17 Same old drill day. Regt. stood for taking of a picture.

JAN. 18 Regt. received tractors today probably will get rid of some horses.

JAN. 19 In eve. Tuffy Brons and I worked on R-H.

JAN. 20 The Canadians are here for a boxing tournament. I have been busy all day endeavoring to entertain those given this battery. In afternoon the wrestling meet was won by the Yanks every fall. In the eve. there were four fine bouts one of which the Canadians won. In the eve four of them stayed in our room. We doubled up so as to accommodate them. They were fine fellows and interesting in conversation. Their talk is the same as ours, and the accent is similar, one can not tell the difference between us except in uniform. Their uniforms have brass buttons and are certainly snappy though their baggy trousers are not so good looking as ours.

JAN. 21 | We woke the Canucks for breakfast after we stood reveille. They say our food is better than theirs, but I don't believe any soldier. at least they are allowed to get as many parcels from home as are sent while we are allowed none.

At 7 I was told that I had a one day pass to visit Bonn and see the Amer-Canadian ball game, so I went down to hdq rgt. with Nitz and we piled in a truck and made the journey to Bonn up the Rhine valley. The majestic old stream deserves its reputation for its graceful curves around the palisades with fine cities dotting the banks and bridges spanning the stream are among the finest in the world.

After reaching Bonn Walter and I took a car for Cologne where we spent a few hours roaming around visiting the great cathedral the fine theater and places of interest. A thing which impressed me was the department stores they are of artistic construction being more like museums than stores and they are modern inside.

The British are of course running the town. They are more commanding and domineering than we and have less patience with the Germans than we which I believe is a good thing, for at heart these civilians are still Huns and would support the Kaiser if he should come back after we leave, I believe.

In the evening we returned to Bonn with the Canadians. I did not have time to look up the friends who had visited us but went to the Stadt theatre where the Canadian 2d div was giving a show. I enjoyed it very much.

Later in the evening Walt and I picked up Louie in a cafe. Being an Indian and he was the attraction of the place and we had difficulty in getting him away so missed the 8 train. But we went to the station and found that one went at 12:45 we waited in a Canadian rest house a place where men on leave are fed and may sleep between train times.

The 2 Canadians who ran the place (cooks) were kind to us feeding us and offering us tea every two minutes.

We had a delightful time in talking over the days on the front and our feelings and experiences were strangely alike. They of course hate the Germans, as the Kaiser statue in the public square showes by the missing helmet spike and nose. They tell of the crusifiction of one of their sergeants, and tell of the terrible stories told by the returned prisoners of war from Germany. These prisoners were starved and beaten and hissed by the civilians as well as the guards. The Belgians suffered worse than any other people during the war from the inhuman treatment by the Huns military machine. The rationing was as bad in Germany as anywhere else however. Even here in Bonn fats meat butter were unobtainable and even dogs were eaten.

In Belgium when German man or officer came down the sidewalk a Belgian had to step off the walk make an about face and take off his hat if a woman bow. The Hun did not of course return the salutation. In Germany a person were allowed to buy a small loaf of bread a week. It was marked in several parts. Inspectors came into a home at will and if a person had taken a slice of his bread meant for the next day he was either sent to jail or paid a large fine. The Kaiser and pals were about the only people who had their cellars filled with food.

During the course of our conversation I learned more of the British and Canadians and their armies than I had ever known. One had served in the Kings guard in London for eight years before he went to Canada. He believed in the English system of govt. and thot the King a blessing because of his creating a bond of union throughout the Empire; though his actual power was negligable. He said the land of manners and aristocracy and blood was England while the land of money was America. He preferred America saying that his two brothers and three sisters had tried every means to get him to return to his home in London, where he was a cockney. I told him he didn't have the cockney dialect but he said that cockney designated a part of London and the difference in speech was in education. King Edward was a cockney he said having been born in Buckingham palace in the cockney district.

We boarded our train at 12:45 getting in a second-class coach which was crowded even women sitting on the floor bench. These girls were especially hospitable being very willing to accept Louie's embraces as well as others.

We got off at Roumogen because the train was bound for Coblenz and we found that there would be no train for Neuenahr before 5:45 a.m. so we decided to walk the 11 or 15 kilos. We started out at a fast clip which lasted about eight kilos then rested a minute and were off to the finis. The last kilos were awful because we had been walking all day anyway and our legs were sore and we were very tired. But we stuck it out and reached our beds at 4:30.

JAN. 22

It was rather hard to make reville at 6:30 but I did it, though I was sleepy all day. Parade at 1:30. Hit the hay before taps. Pay day.

JAN. 23

Took a bath this morning and put on my new trousers I am now newly equipped having discarded the trousers I got at Chateau Thierry in fact I havent found a cootie on myself for three weeks so they must have gone.

Capt. Barbour returned to the bat. after a two weeks trip to France.

JAN.

24

Parade in afternoon In evening heard "Mignon" by a German grand opera Co. which I must admit I did not enjoy very much.

JAN.

25

Usual Sat. inspection this morning.

JAN.

26

Had an interview with the colonel today and he encouraged me about R.H. and gave his sanction.

JAN.

27

Seventy of us from the battery went on pass today to Coblenz. A special train of U.S. box cars starting from Ahrweiler carried the permissions of the entire brigade. We followed the Ahr valley to Sinzig where we came into the Rhein valley. Down to Andernach the valley was deep with palisades and great hills forming the boundries. But from Andernach to Coblenz our route was through level country almost as flat as our western country.

Crossing the Mosel we came into Coblenz where the bridge head which the American army is holding is located. A pontoon and two other bridges span the Rhein here. We crossed the middle bridge setting foot on this east bank of the Rhein at Ehrenbreitstein. On the Coblenz side of the bridge is the great palace of the Kaiser. Bill had these fine homes all over Germany and this was one of the finest. The Americans hold church in one end of it. The Kaiser also had a wonderful castle up the river. It is filled with art treasures (Stolzenfels)

At the point where the Mosel empties into the Rhein there is a massive statue of William I. More at the center of the city is the Kaiser Wilhelm ring which a year ago was alive with flags in honor of Bill's birthday. Today his 60th birthday sees American soldiers promenading about the streets and the few flags in evidence were American.

I stopped into an art shop and bought some fine engravings scenes of Bonn Cologne, and Coblenz and some of the authors of the war. The old salesman thot surely that I was an admirer of the Kaiser because I was buying his picture and he took occasion to remark that it was the Kaiser's birthday. "A poor man," he said I told him that I supposed he was having a tough time in his palace in Holland and I understood he had taken only 27,000,000 marks with him. But the old boy only said that Bill didn't start the war.

Coming down one of the main thoroughfares we came across a small display window in which was a cartoon from a German paper. It represented the Allies as outside the door of Germany with hunger and anarchy as his companions and ready to batter down the door to admit them. Naturally my blood boiled at the insulting picture and with a blow of my elbow I shattered the glass, which crashed to the walk, and tore out the offensive picture.

I was expecting to have to make a run for it if the M.P. on the corner saw it but he was busy directing traffic. Everybody stopped on the street and one German started in my direction but when I went out to meet him he walked on.

We had a good supper at the Union restaurant, which served only men on leave and then attended a show at the Y. theater, while there we stepped in on an impromptu dance and I danced with a real American girl for the first time since August 1917.

We were scheduled to leave the station at 10 p.m. but were delayed until 11:15 and it was mighty cold in the box cars too. The trip was of course cold and rough and being sleepy also, we crabbed all the way to Neuenahr, everybody vowing never to accept a day's leave again, but as I think of the sleepless nights we spent on the front and in hiking in northern France I can see that this short rail journey was a cinch in comparison. But it is human nature to always want conditions bettered We now have beds and plenty to eat yet we crab. When I think of days on the front I hardly see how we stood it. Lots of fellows say they couldn't go thru it again but if it is necessary one can stand almost anything. One could not realize what a soldier passed through during the war without being one himself.

| JAN. 28 | Signed pay roll. We are now getting fine bread from the new division bakery here, in fact our food is better and more plentiful than ever before. The commercial side of the Boche is shown not only by their sales of the iron cross, but now they are selling |

a cigar labelled Rainbow division.

| JAN. 29 | In evening saw 150 FA band in Hoosier Follies. The camouflage chorus girls were [enthusiastically] received. Fink refused reserve commis because he is an alien. |

| JAN. 30 | Moved switchboard from our room to office so we will not have to tend to it any longer, but I am on battery guard tonight. Ushered at Deutsch entertainment for soldiers at Kurtheater tonight. |

JAN.
31

On guard today, so had some time to write letters and I mailed about a dozen to the folks and friends.

At noon we turned in our pistols and ammunition. We no longer will carry them as in the past when we were ordered never to appear without them. Tonight we saw Douglas Fairbanks in a movie which was good.

FEB.
1

Usual weekly inspection. Col [Robert H.] Tyndall has gone to France on pass and Lieut Col now coming has made us out quite a strenuous schedule.

FEB.
2

February 2. Drove truck this morning. Slayman has returned with more tractors and trucks and it seems that we will soon displace all horses if we stay here long enough.

FEB.
3

Motor school morning as usual. Afternoon on horse line.

FEB.
4

Hitched harnessed and pulled out today as of old going to posits. facing Rhein, where we went through a play war.

FEB.
5

[no entry]

FEB.
6

Motor school in morning. Horse line evening.

National Archives

Theater, Neuenahr (Bad Neuenahr-Ahrweiler), Germany. The theater was occupied by the 167th and 168th Ambulance Companies during the American occupation.

FEB. 7

On guard last night and today.

FEB. 8

Inspection this morning. Snow now is that we embark at Rotterdam on Feb. 16 for home. Of course we dont put much faith in report but it sounds good anyway.

Sent in last of mms of R.H and illustrations by Cottingham.

FEB. 12

[Entry out of order in diary.] Aside from grooming and formations we now spend some time in practicing sempaphore. We never used it on the war but _____

FEB. 10

On guard. At 2:30 we stood guard mount, a formal military display, accompanied by band.

It is pretty cold during small hours of morning posting guards.

FEB.

11

Neuenahr is now a rest area for div. where men come on one day passes. At last the YMCA is doing something. They have taken over casino, theater, restaurant and canteen.

FEB.

9

[Entry out of order in diary.] Entire Rgt. attended memorial service for T.R. [Theodore Roosevelt] in Kur theater. Chaplin Nash gave a fine talk upon the type of man he was and on his accomplishments.

FEB.

13

We now have four trucks and four tractors which are intended to replace the horses but we still have the latter.

FEB.

14

In the next two days we are to prepare for an inspection from C in C.

FEB.

15

Saw movies and stills of the division. They were pretty good, tho giving little actual battle scenes. Picture of Menhor [Maj. Gen. Charles T. Menoher] was cheered more than that of [Secretary of War Newton D.] Baker and [Gen. John J.] Pershing combined.

FEB.

16

Sunday.

The inspection and review by Gen. Pershing was called off, so a battery inspection was held.

FEB.

17

A little German school boy who came from Africa to attend high school here in 1914 came over to see us. He is a wonderful student and is mastering the English language, speaking it with a perfect pronunciation.

Signalling practice took up part of day.

FEB. 18

Drove one of the new tractors for the first time today They are Holts with Reo engines and are powerful brutes armoured and treaded just like tanks.

Visited German school for a while today during the geography lesson the different colonies were mentioned and when ex-German colonies were mentioned the kids enjoyed the joke as much as I and of course all turned to look at me.

FEB. 19

Regiment began target practice today and the valley resounds with the explosions. Sounds like old times.

Lt. Vick today gave Sgt Fink and Marsh his idea of the relation of officers and enlisted men of the army. He said "you are mere men while we are gentlemen." When asked about the men promoted to officers from ranks he said "Oh! you can often find a diamond in the rough."

Corps general [C. H.] Muir, division gen. Flagler and brigade general [George C.] gatley were in town today looking over the regiment to see if we were sufficiently motorized to allow us to turn in horses.

FEB. 20

I spent day in obtaining information on men of battery killed in action or died of wounds for a headquarters report.

FEB. 21

Usual day on picket line but varied by a couple of hours in practicing semaphore in afternoon.

Morning attended very enlightening and interesting demonstration—described in detail on another page.

FEB. 22

George's and my birthday so we have a part of the day off in honor of it.

Of course I got a beating (23 licks[)] at reville, but rest of day passed without event until eve when I was called to Skippers room and he asked if I wanted a pass 7 days to Aix les Bains of course I did and so went out to find Louie who is going with me. He is a full blooded Indian and has made a good soldier (is a sgt) and since we went thro this thing from the start I know we'll have a good time on leave together tho I expect to have to take care of him when the fire water gets plentiful.

He was at the corner bookstore as usual talking to the frauline, whom he likes so much that he goes in to see her every night and always comes away with post cards or something I'll bet he has a room ful now.

At any rate he agreed to go if we could get some money and on this mission, It didn't take long to raise the 500F he wanted so we are all set to go tomorrow.

An indefatigable sightseer, Elmer Sherwood seized the opportunity to go on leave to France. The trip to the old town of Annecy was, of course, by train and was long but fairly pleasant, albeit in crowded third-class coaches. Once there Sherwood saw the sights with much interest and filled his travel diary with information that he probably heard from others or read in a guidebook. The youth from Linton had been taken with the historic past in Neuenahr, and now everything he heard or was told about Annecy appeared worth writing about. In the course of the leave he went to Chamonix and saw the Alps, including Mont Blanc.

In *Rainbow Hoosier* and *Diary of a Rainbow Veteran* he did not mention Annecy. *Rainbow Hoosier* dealt with the occupation but omitted his leave, and the *Diary of a Rainbow Veteran* ended with the armistice. The Annecy diary, now in the Lilly Library, appears in this chapter and chapter eleven.

FEB. 23 After going thru a bunch of red tape from a physical exam to checking up on equipment, Louie, Marsh, and I reported to regt. hdq. at 3:30 and waited until 5:00 when we loaded in quads and started on a wild ride to Coblenz via the Rhine road. It was a pleasant night cold enough to make an overcoat feel good. We made good speed arriving in Coblenz at 7:10 where we lined up in front of the RR station until 11 pm when we boarded our train.

During the wait we saw Lieut Woods, a one time officer of B. bat, now in the army RR corps. He showed us how to get some food at Red Cross canteen. We went in and were served by the RC ladies who were working like slaves to appease the hunger of so many Yanks.

There are a great bunch of fellows on pass from the A of O every division being represented. We are in third class coaches which are comfortable enough five in our compartment Sgt. Harry Shireman medico Glen Crawford Hdq. Co, Sgt. Island, Corp Marsh and self B. Bat. There are no cushions (bare board) on the seats but the compartment is more roomy than those of the French railroad coaches.

Red Cross women ("RC ladies") and troops. The Red Cross, Salvation Army, YMCA, and the Knights of Columbus provided a plethora of services to soldiers at home and overseas.

FEB. 24 After a night of trying to sleep sitting on the benches we tumbled out at 4:30 am to get some coffee and sandwiches from the Red Cross canteen at Trier.

I suppose our ten weeks in Neuenahr have spoiled us for such travel for we used to sleep like logs in the box cars. However after eating, and with the coming of daylight we felt fine again.

This morning we passed thru Kurthaus, Thionville, and Hangondange, following the Moselle river I believe, for a time. About Hangondange were enormous industrial plants, steele and iron foundries and ore mines. Now we came to Metz, capital of Lorraine many French soldiers were to be seen everywhere, unarmed. The change after riddence of the Huns is typified by the repainted signs which are now printed bearing French words in place of German words. About the city are great railroad yards and manufacturing plants. While south and west it is surrounded by level farming lands.

The city is a fortified one and the ancient walls are still standing modernized. A canal on one side and a river another are a natural protection being spanned only by fortified bridges. The streets of the city are broad and the buildings generally well constructed. Several church spires tower above the other buildings.

Outside the city I have seen some trenches dug for reserve positions no doubt. Beginning at Ars-Moselle we can begin to see the effects of arial bombs and long range guns. Shell holes are numerous. This territory came within range of our heavies after the St. Mihiel operation. The station at Noveant was almost completely demolished.

From this time on we passed through the territory which had changed hands during the war. Near Pagtry began the trenches, barbed wire defenses and camouflaged roads. Vandres was destroyed, a former no mans land with torn up bridges and roads dugouts about. Coming as we do from an unscathed land (Germany) these scenes burst into our view giving us fresh sensations of horror as the first sight of them did a year ago, when we entered the lines in Lorraine (not many miles from here) for the first time.

Pont-A-Mousson, partially destroyed marked the far point of German advance here and according to a doughboy stationed here the 90th div. advanced four miles n.w. at the time of our advance at St. Mihil. A mademoselle was selling oranges at the station, the first we have eaten for a long time. Again we are in the peaceful country where there are no visible signs of war.

Our route followed a barge canal between Belleville and Toul. It was full of large barges, some stationary and others moving being pulled by a team of horses, led by a man or woman. The progress is exceedingly slow and the great barge seems just to barely move, but the French don't believe in hurrying thru life anyway so they don't notice the time it takes.

Two Frogs rode in our compartment a few miles to Toul. One is going home to Paree being discouraged and the other is a permissionare both happy of course and telling us all that they are going to do to have a good time. I notice that the French along the route appear as during the war slow and blasé. We have also seen some of the Annamites workmen as well as Italians, the latter on a train also, however they are homeward bound. They had an American flag with their own on one car. They surely do worship America.

War material is as much in evidence as during the war, being in piles and masses. There are many guns awaiting transportation.

I can't forget the last time I passed thru Toul. It was on a terrible hike, the toughest I believe we ever took, for we were being rushed with all speed to the St. Mihil drive. It was dark when we passed Neufchateau. We were wiser tonight and lay our blankets on the floor where we got some sleep.

FEB. 25 | The train stopped this morning at Is-sur-Tille, famous American camp. Here we got a cup of coffee and slice of bread and were off again, passing Dijon, a large city.

We have made poor speed so far, having had one car to get off the track but will probably get to Aix this evening. On U.S. trains we would have been there long ago.

We seem to be curiosities, our German train giving us away and the sign which reads Leave Train Coblenz to Aix-Les-Bains. At Toul a red cross nurse questioned me about Germany, and seemed very much concerned for fear we were being affected by the Hun propaganda.

It is a common expression among the fellows for sport to yell "Who won the war?" and in presence of YMCA workers or MP's to give their organization as the answer; but at one stop an MP beat the jester to the answer and replied We did_____by keeping you up to the front.

The three of us from Bat. B. had for rations two lo[a]ves of bread and two cans of beans. Red had a can of woolie and "Doc" Sherman had nothing. This didn't amount to much for three days but we made out, with aid of the two coffee stops and what we were able to buy at the stations. It was a _____ job to get the stuff though, for as soon as the train pulled up to a station a mob would jump off the train and rush the stands, so a fellow was lucky if he bought anything before the train pulled out. Louie always managed to buy a little vin rouge however.

Our meager rations reminded me of the old woman going East, whom Mr. Humphreys used to tell about. He said she had three or four baskets full of food (chicken etc) and about every five minutes she would bring out the hoard of food and begin eating, in fact her trip was one long feast, he said. We were not that lucky so when we arrived at our destination we were half starved.

After leaving Dijon we passed St-Jean-de-Losne Surre, Nabilly, Simard, Louhans, and St. Amour. It has been raining for some time and the country is flooded, especially about Louhans where part of the town streets resembled canals.

We are now in the beautiful country of Savoie among the foot hills of the Alps. Bourg is the largest city hereabout and is built somewhat on the style of some california towns red tiled roofs etc. Passing Ambrauy-Praily and Amberieu we come into a great valley. On either side of us rise mountains almost all of them bald at the peaks rising in solid rocky precipices to a great heighth. A small river runs to our side. The French have the hillsides covered with vineyards in places but do not terrace them as the Germans do.

The route is a wonderland of scenic beauty even more beautiful than the Rhine valley. On the way past Lenay, Rossallin, Vixieu Grand, Antemare and Culoz our road bed passed through three mountains in some great tunnels. We are running on the bank of a great crystal lake which nestles among the snow-capped mountains.

At Aix-les-Bains the train stopped an hour, here we talked to the British aboard a train bound for Brest and home. They came from Mesopotamia where they went in 1915 and all of them say they are "fed up" of army life and war and glad to get back.

The leave center has been moved from Aix on account of the influenza to Annecy, so after delay we left Aix and made a snails progress to Annecy, which we reached at 7 p.m.[1] We lined up at the station with our packs and marched to headquarters passing the details of leave men who are going out. They were of the 6th div. and the boys jibed them with "Have a look at some real soldiers, and Who won the war" etc. Everybody was yelling and I guess the natives thought something was going to happen, for they lined the streets and helped us make noise.

After the miserable hike to headquarters we entered the building, stood a physical examination signed cards and went through other red tape until finally we were allowed to march to our hotels. Ours is the "Mont Blanck" and we have good beds. Before retiring we bought a supper and attended a vaudeville show at Y.

FEB.
26

Arose at 8 bells and after making our toilets went down for breakfast which consisted of coffee bread and jam. We ordered extra some eggs. Our hotel bill including meals are paid for by Uncle Sam, but of course extras are up to us.

We went over the Y hut[2] and at 10 am one of the secretaries took us over to visit the foundry and to hear the victory bell "Joan of Arc" ring. This is the largest bell in the world, since the Bell of Moscow has been destroyed. The latter bell was of no use any way owing to the great hole in it. The bell's dimensions are wt. 22 tons. Hgt. 10½ ft circumf 29½ ft. Diam. 10½ ft and it is to be rung in the Rouen cathedral the moment peace is signed being the official and first bell to ring out the glad tidings. The truth however is that the Americans were the first to ring it. We got on the ropes and made the old boy resound in thunderous peals. It was almost as deafening as the roar of the guns opening up a big drive but was a fine tone of course.

We saw in the foundry bells from many lands to be recast notably one from China another from Alsace-Lorraine which the Boches had rung until it bursted when they captured the territory in 1870. Now the French are having it recast so that they may ring it until it bursts again (to get it back on the Boche)[.]

Some new bells were destined for South America (Peru) 3 and Canada. There was also a set of chimes 28 bells for the Rouen cathedral also. One of the boys played the Star Spangled banner on it and M. Pa played La Marseille and other compositions which brought out the wonderful tones of the bells.

We saw bells being cast and in other stages of construction. It is characteristic of the French that this most famous plant for making bells in the world is only a small one, going in for quality rather than quantity The two brothers members of a family of bell makers ages old in reputation seem to be an ideal pair one is the manufacturer while—the other is the artist they show it in appearance also. They do not seem to be more than comfortably situated financially though they got 90,000 francs for the famous victory bell.

In the afternoon I visited some art shops and bought a few pictures and souvenires three of them engravings of the town scenes. Later went to

Y for an afternoon dance with real American girls. Jane Wilhoite ("Georgia") La Grange Georgia. (Y.M.C.A. address 12 Rue d'Agresseau, Paris[)].

FEB. 27

Arose in time this morning to get to the Hut before Mr Hagen and party had started on the trip (10 bells) and so joined them. He pointed out the spots of interest first monument to Eugéne Sue author of The Wandering Jew, which work was written at Annecy. We then visited the Marie in which the museum is located. Here we saw many specimens of Roman work which had been dug up from the site of the old Roman town located near here on the plain of Finis, between Geneva and Cran. It was called Boutae. The village was pillaged and burnt by invaders and was only rebuilt in IX century, when the name Annisiacum was given it—origin of modern name of course.

Through the ages the town has been a battle place of kings and nobles until upon annex[at]ion to France from Italy it was made the administrative center of the dept. of Haute-Savoie. In 1556, says the guide, Eustache Chappuis, Charles the fifths' ambassador, founded a flourishing grammer school, St. Francis and jurist Antoine Favre inst[it]uted the Académie Florimontane 1606. We viewed the ancient building with interest it being a fine example of gothic architecture.

The Thiou river flows from Lac D'Annecy through the town (13000 pop) and into it many subterranean canals, which emerge from beneath various streets flow. They unite and form the Flier near the bridge of Cran.

The streets of the town in the old district (ie Ste Claire St.) are peculiar in that the buildings are built over the walks in great arches. These covered walks and passages were used in the olden times in street fighting.

The opponents sought some protection behind the arches and when he wanted to get away he would disappear into one of the many passage ways and come out probably unobserved in some other street possibly in another part of town.

We then visited an old historic castle which had later become a prison. When it was built centuries ago it was the acme of luxury but today it is as forbidding as a dug out.

Where once banquets were held, historical societies meet to preserve history and relics of this locality I saw J.P. Morgan's picture upon the wall and noted that he was a member of the society. Many relics of Italian occupation are here as well as the old chains etc used in the prison period. A passage underground leads to the castle up on the hill from this old towered building. [The following was apparently added by Sherwood at a later time.] Savoy obtained by French in nineteenth century[.]

We walked up the hill thru ancient narrow streets which have never been altered even the buildings are as they were centuries ago, characteristic of certain class of the French people.

A great castle dominates the surrounding country from this hill It now holds four hundred german officers, whom we saw exercising in the court-yard.

While on the hill we visited the large nunnery. When a girl enters it she never comes out. In it were the skeletons of Saint Francis and of Madame de Chantal in gilt shrines. About the skeletons have been moulded human forms from some sort of plaster and they do look like real corpses, not very pleasant I thought.

Had lunch at Y canteen. Here we can get excellent food at nominal cost and it is served by real American girls. One of them especially attracted me black hair and eyes and with a smile for everybody. She handled the coffee and in a sweet voice she would ask sugar and cream? There were several guys hanging around the counter to hear her ask that I suppose.

Anyway I saw her at tea "Hotel Angleterre" and danced with her, inci-dentally making a date for the theater. I felt like a kid when I asked her; embarrassed I suppose, because of the fact that I hadn't done such a thing since 1917—It is good to associate again with this sort of girls after being used to mademoselles—

Attended show with Margaret Whitehead and afterward saw her home. She is a graduate of Wisconsin where she was a Theta and of course is very interesting. The show was a wild west Mellerdramer staged by our own tal-ent hence very rotten.

FEB. 28 | Left station of Annecy at 9 this morning on train for Chamonix with several other Yanks. The route was through an especially beautiful country. Coming from the smaller mountains and foot hills to the greatest of the Alps.

At Saint Gervais we changed trains and as I had forgotten my creden-tials I was glad to meet an MP from Indianapolis who had been a student at Purdue and who knew many people I knew. His name was Dixon 228 MP. Co. and since he was going to Chamonix also we travelled together and he being more familiar with this part of France pointed out the points of interest. It snowed today and the Alps look most beautiful covered with the white blankets. It is clearing up and we can now see the peaks of some though they are among the clouds.

The Glacier des Bossons, one of the greatest in the world, comes plainly within our view and we can see a party of Yanks climbing over it. The great mountains on our right are all disignated by the name Mont-Blanc It is a range, but from Chamonix we can see Mt Blanc proper, the highest mountain in Europe.

In Chamonix one of the famous resorts of Europe we had only two hours to spend. It is also a leave center and the greatest hotel is run by the Y. It is a wonderful palace and we visited it for lunch. After which we took a walk up the way to get a better view of Mt. Blanc. The elevation is very great even here and one gets short of breath when walking, but many are out on snow shoes and skis having a jolly time.

I made the return trip to Annecy with some regret because I liked Chamonix and its surroundings and surely am going to return there some day.

On the return journey I happened to get in the same compartment with a M. Giraud of Paris, who has a home also in Chamonix. He had learned English and was very anxious to talk to me. He was very jolly though a rather old man, in fact he reminded me very much of Dad in many ways. He said that he has been a friend of a Mr. Robinson of Westinghouse Co who is now in Texas and he thought it such a joke that the American was a tetotler, telling me about the time when he had offered R. some red lemonade but R refused thinking it camouflaged wine.

A French soldier in our compartment began groaning presently and G said that he evidently wasn't a tetotler which was the truth. I offered G some of my American candy which he liked very much. He showed me pictures of his homes and told how he had ridden over Europe on a bicycle and queer enough he had visited Neuenahr and could tell me about the places I was familiar with there. He said that the Alps where I had been were far better and more beautiful than in Switzerland. From any of the mountains the boundaries of Italy, France and Switzerland can be seen.

Presently M Giraud brought out one of his baskets and set up a little heater in which he boiled water (alcohol burner) and cooked an egg. He wished me to dine with him but I assured him that I had eaten at Chamonix, but he insisted upon my tasting his special wine which indeed tasted very good to me though I taste them seldom.

11 | Paris
(FEBRUARY–MARCH 1919)

Whether due to boredom or the result of a challenge laid down by Margaret Whitehead, Elmer Sherwood took a train to Paris. It was an impulse, and he was absent without leave (AWOL).

FEB. 28

Upon arrival at Annecy I bade him [M. Giraud] goodby and went directly to the Y canteen. I was drinking a cup of chocolate when Margaret came over to me and asked why I hadn't gone to Paris.

The day before I had told her that I was going to see Paris and she told me that the train to Chamonix would be the one but I found that in going there I had gone away from instead of toward Paris. I explained this and she said just the same that is the train and if you want to get it you have five minutes yet for it stops here a half hour for search owing to the fact that it comes from the Swiss border and has to be examined by the customs officials.

I ran for it eluding the station guards, because we are not allowed to leave the town at night. But I got into a little cubby hole, where the conductor sits when off duty. I pulled down the blind but it wouldn't stay down so I had to hold it and hold the door shut at the same time so that no M.P. could arrest me. I could see through the key hole and believe me I sweat some when I saw one M.P. come in at Aix-les-Bains and try to open the door I was holding; but I held it shut and he left thinking it was locked I suppose.

The trainmen came in three times for some articles and each time I saw him coming I allowed the door to open and stayed behind it as it opened. But on the third time he discovered me behind the door and he addressed me in rapid fire French, but I simply vamoosed. I was practically safe anyway now for we were under full speed on the way to Paree. But all compartments were full so I had to stand up, however I wanted to stay awake as I expected the MPs to search the train at the important stops so each time we came to a stop I went to the toilet and locked the door until we had pulled out of the station.

MAR.
1

I was glad when morning came and warmer temperature succeeded the chilly night air. Then I noticed by the map and time table that we were nearing the metropolis. Our route had included:

Aix-les-Bains,	Lournus,
Culos,	Chalons-Sur-Saone,
Amberien,	Dijon,
St Jean L. V.,	Tonnerre,
Bourg,	Joigny, Sens,
Macon,	Montereau.

As we approached the city I began looking for an opportunity to jump off so as to avoid station guards but had little chance and the first thing I knew we were in the Gare de Lyon; but I hopped off before we had gotten into the shed and dodged behind some box cars. Then I boldly walked out of a gate guarded by two French soldiers but supposing I had business there they did not challenge me.

I then walked through a lumber yard into the street paralleling the Seine walking past Notre-Dame cathedral and near here I got a street car and rode the short distance to the Opera square, where I hailed a taxi and found out by the drivers curt reply that it was lunch time and he for one was going to eat. With this pleasing introduction to the Paris taxi driver in mind I visited a restaurant myself.

After lunch I got a taxi and rode about "seeing things" until we had a blow out, so I wasn't in a mood to tarry and seeing the indicator at a franc and fraction handed the driver two francs but just then the indicator clicked to two and a fraction because he was monkeying with the wheel I suppose and he demanded another franc. Imagine him getting it from a soldier and a Yank at that.

I walked about for a while past the Madelenie and up the theater district always keeping clear of American M.P.'s. I would often times have to cross the streets but in crowds there was little danger and I even began to enjoy the flavor of the risk I was taking, still I couldn't bear to dwell upon what would happen if I were caught and asked for a pass. Of course my pass called for Annecy and not Paris, which was a restricted district, which we were not permitted to visit. So the consequence would probably have been imprisonment until a courtmartial then I might have been sent to a labor battalion and withdrawn from the 150 F.A. hence would not be allowed to return with the div. in April. But I acted as if I belonged in Paris and was luckey enough to get away with it.

After seeing the Hotel-De-Ville I walked down the Rue de Rivoli to the Jardin des Tuiteries [Tuileries] where there were numberless captured German cannon about the Obelisque in Place de la Concorde and other monuments. From here one can see the wonderful Arc de Triomphe up the Avenue des Champs Elysées. Then I turned my steps up through the garden to the Tuileries. I believe I have never seen such a fine group of buildings with such wonderfully arranged gardens filled with artistic monuments as this place. I have always admired Washington as a fine and artistic city but realize now that it will take years to bring it up to the high artistic plane upon which Paris is. To appreciate the hight of French accomplishment in architecture, art and industry one must see Paris. It is all that I expected and more. I will never be satisfied until I come back again to spend a longer time.

I entered the Louvre then and spent some pleasant hours among the finest art treasures of the world. The Winged Victory and Venus de Milo were among the many I recognized from the pictures and copies I had seen. I haven't the training to fully appreciate such works of art, yet I was impressed by their beauty as interpretations of mortals. Then I visited the halls filled with paintings, noting especially those by the artists Rubens, Ribot and Millet of whom I was more familiar, Still there were other canvasses by less famous ones, which were as good. I can now easily realize why to be a critic and judge a person must spend his life in the study of art.

Coming out of the Louvre to the Quai I saw a car marked Versailles and decided to go out to the palace so boarded it.

We passed the petit-palais, grand palais and palais and jardins du Trocadero. The avenue President Wilson was here and of course I saw it with interest. Across the Seine we had passed the Palais de L'institut, Gare Orleans, Chambre des Députés along the Quai d'Orsay. When we passed the monstrous Eiffel tower and palais Trocadero I knew we were in the old World's fair site. The great ferris wheel could also be seen in the distance.

Coming into the limits of Versailles I noticed the great numbers of military motor cars and trucks parked in the streets. I believe they were to be auctioned off soon.

At the old hotel de Ville we got off the car and I directed my steps to the magnificent palace entering the gate to the grounds and walking up between the rows of great statues to the colossel one of the emperor.

I was impressed as much by the vastness of the palace as by its architecture and the nicety of arrangement of its buildings. These wings and parts of the palace buildings varied in their inner magnificence as well as on the outside. Some have not been well taken care of and in fact are closed and disregarded, dirty disorderly torn up but other halls are in fine condition and just as beautiful as when occupied by royalty. Now of course it resembles a museum more than then with more statuary and exhibits than when used as a home.

But tho I was impressed by the exterior and interior of the palace and the court grounds in front, which by the way contained also a number of captured cannon I was awed by the view of the park and gardens which greeted me as I stepped from the palace itself into, the back yard as it were. The palace itself is on elevated ground overlooking the surrounding grounds. And the roads walks steps lead from the group of buildings to the finest garden I ever expect to see. Hedges, evergreen trees, gardens grass plots all are arranged with such a nicety of balance.

Great walks lead among large trees being bordered with rows of statues, there must be thousands in the park, At the sides of the walks and behind the statues, among the trees nature is allowed to run its course and it is simply a wild forest, but the walk leads to a great fountain. From this center, there are hundreds of them, one may look in any direction and select a walk, which in every case will lead to other fountains.

I kept this up, determined to walk to the limits until I came to the banks of a large lake, about which of course were various statues. And I saw beyond what seemed to be endless walks, so as it was getting dusky I decided to turn back. This was where my trouble came about, for I was now within sight of the great palace and hadn't paid any attention to direction, so I took a path and kept walking or rather wandering, Surely I had walked miles and miles and still did not know where the palace was yet I knew I was in no wilderness, for the ever present statues were still to be seen along the paths, so I kept going and came finally to a gate. I stepped onto the walk and found that I was in the city of Versailles again, though I could not swear yet what the location of the palace was.

I was tired and hungry so stopped in a restaurant and got a good supper, while there a party of American soldiers came in and began a conversation with me. I found out that they were not MP's so I told them that I was A.W.O.L and they asked me if I knew that I was now out of the Paris limits. I hadn't thought of that and now I had to elude the M.P's to get back again and this the fellows assured me would be a hard job for one of them had just got out of the guard house where he had served three weeks for going to Paris without pass. And he said it was filled with soldiers, YMCA and K of C men, and officers up to general.[1] So they told me the best way to go and I got a car destined for the Invalides.

On the car I met a poilu who had been discharged from the army this day and he took me in tow. We got of[f] the car and walked fast in the erand, passing a couple of M.P's, and then got the subway. Of course it was easy then to get to any part of the city. I went to the opera not thinking about the day being Sunday. but I found there was to be no performance after I had entered the house. The staircase of the opera is magnificent of marble and gilt.

Then I visited the Opera Comique and found it likewise dark so I decided to promenade along the boulevard. The avenue was thronged mainly by beautiful women who seemed to think it perfectly proper to wear their skirts to the knees. I think Paris is celebrated justly concerning the beauty of its women for I thot they were all beauties. Of course the style of dress might have had something to do with their attractive appearance, but I do believe that the saying is true that all the pretty French girls flock to Paris.

Naturally they were quite bold and in the course of the evening many different madamoselles *escorted* me. Their laxity of morals did not seem to detract from their brightness, for they were witty and delighted to talk the little American they knew. However when they would state their mission I would look at my wrist watch and say that I had to make a train at the Gare de Lyon toot sweet, which of course caused us to take a sad departure. I must confess that I did enjoy these strange girls. However the fact was that I decided to leave tonight, for if I had stayed a day longer I might have found the place so attractive that I would not have gotten out in time to get the leave train back.

So I walked to the Gare de Lyon at midnight and getting into the sheds I found a box car in which I slept until my train was about due to leave. I had a time table so knew how to get my train and after my long training in box cars I found this no draw back.

MAR. 2

At six the train I wanted pulled in and I boarded it, keeping under cover until it pulled out. Then I washed and went to a first class compartment. Owing to my unusual method of travel and being an American soldier I was not asked for fare. (In France tickets are collected at the stations)

In my compartment was a major, two lieuts, and a Frenchman wife and child. Everyone was friendly, and the major especially conversed with me, of course I felt as good as he, for he was of a division which hadn't seen service, and of course in my estimation a private with two service stripes for line duty is superior to a general without any. Of course I say that is my opinion, from which one may gather that the men, who did the fighting do not underestimate themselves.

But really I am thankful that not only the teaching and example of Mom and Dad and sisters but the hard knocks of army life, have made me feel at ease in any company. It is good to feel equal (tho never superior) to others, then conversation with anyone is interesting and entertaining. I am sure that I would enjoy talking to the president today whereas in the past I would have been pained by embarassment.

At breakfast in the diner I sat at a table with a gentleman from Scotland, one from London, and one from the States. And we talked of many and various things including travel, world affairs and the situation along the Rhein.

I ate with a French officer and two ladies. The food was very good but when the waitress demanded my bread ticket I couldn't produce but the lady opposite came to the rescue and bought another piece with her ticket. The other lady carried an extra piece in her pocket book I noticed. The bread is much better now than during the war. It is white and the crust is crisp, being baked in extremely long and narrow loaves.

In the evening we came to Lyon where I had to change trains, since the one I was on was going to Nice. I couldn't get by the guard to get to the city so I took a train and arrived at Chambre where I expected to get a train for Aix, but I was too late so I spent the night at a hotel in this quaint town which had been the home of Rosseau. The negro American troops now have this place as a leave center and occupied the same hotel I slept in.[2]

MAR. 3
I took a nine o'cloc train for Aix passing through some interesting country en route. Among the Alps near Aix are the passages used by Hannible and Napoleon (not far apart) in their journey across the mountains. We were in Aix only a short time when our train for Annecy arrived.

I jumped off the train before it pulled into Annecy station and walked to my hotel, where I cleaned up. Then I went over to the canteen for dinner and sure enough the girl was there and since she was going down to the tea at hotel Angleterre at three I went along. We stopped at a little ice cream parlor where she questioned me about the trip—etc etc and naturally I told her all about it and told her the story of my life and a few more things among which was the story about how a Hun plane had fallen near me at Exermont and as proof I gave her a souvenir of a piece of wing. But she said "Is this red and blue wing from a Hun plane." Then I had to admit that I had told the wrong story; but she cheered me up by saying she would believe anything I said any way, so of course that called for some sentiments direct from the heart, and ended by the proposition that I should go to Chicago a year hence to see her.

After the afternoon dance we got Bob and Jane to go with us to the theater.

MAR. 4
We were rousted out of bed at nine am to go to headquarters where we passed an inspection and drew travelling rations.

I sleep with Frank and Louie has his bed beside us and we all come in at different times of the night. Last night I came in after the hotel door was locked and had to do a Douglas Fairbanks stunt, climb up to the balcony of second story to get into the building.

Louie was wiser he got in after the door had been opened this morning and Frank was the good boy who went to bed early consequently he pulled Louie and I out this morning to go to hdq.

After the inspection and dinner I went to the canteen and got Margaret, Jane and Bob and we went for a motor boat ride around the lake.

She pointed out the points of interest where St. Bernard had lived and the ruins of the old monastary from which he had sent out his dogs of mercy into the mountains. The place where Rosseau was born and last but not least the home of the artist who painted September Morn and in fact the part of the lake in which the madamoselle had posed but—alas the model was not there to meet our gaze.[3]

The lake is really quite wonderful situated as it is among the mountains and rocky cliffs on one hand. It is of a peculiar purple tint and is so clear that on[e] can see the bottom at great depths.

We were expecting our train to leave at five, but upon returning to shore found that it hadn't come and that we might stay another night, Of course we were happy at this, and not long after we were in the theater seeing the "Comma Ca" company in a clever performance. The jazz band was a wonder too.

After the performance a dance was given so it was early when I hit the hay.

| MAR. 5 | Well at last we are going but on the square I hate to leave. It has been a pleasant week chuck full of interest and enjoyment, and it was so good to see some of the beauty spots of France after having only known the scars. |

I really imagined France a backward, unprogressive, poor land but I have changed my mind completely, now and have a desire to return someday. The French people are as polite and respectful as ever to Americans and the stories that they are tired of us are untrue I observe. In fact I believe they would like to have us stay.

Annecy is the mobalization center for the Blue devils, Chasseurs Alpins, here they have their main barracks drill fields etc and naturally many of them are to be seen on the streets everywhere. No wonder they are good soldiers for they live among these mountains and lead a life in the open.

We didn't get up until eleven. It feels so good to get up when one damn pleases, especially since this was our last chance for a long time. Still we are hopeful for the "Herald" says we are on the April sailing list.

We got a box lunch from the Y canteen to take along. Now after this trip we will have to give the devil his just dues and say that the Y has done us some good. The months and months on the front when the Y did us no good we raved at it and it has become a habit to cuss it and it seems queer to have something good to say about it; but we surely do appreciate the way they have treated us here and though we can't forget those long months that the organization was not in evidence when it was most needed we will forgive to a certain extent. Besides these girls had nothing to do with that.

At five we swung our packs onto our backs and walked to the station where we entrained. This time we rated third class coaches and the same bunch Doc, Red, Frank Louie and I got a compartment.

Doc and Red took the package racks for beds Frank and Louie the seats and I the floor and all seemed to get some rest but Doc says that his leg schreeched like an old hinge.

| MAR. 6 | This morning we passed through Dijon and stopped at Is-sur-Tille where we got some coffee. Unfortunately we had to change trains here and we got one with windows broken out. |

The American casual camp and quartermaster dump is here at Is-sur-Tille. Great railroad yards are filled with locomotives. There are acres of field kitchens etc.

I have a book of Lamb's Tales from Shakespeare and tho it was written for youngsters I have found them interesting.

This evening we are in the country, Hte Marne, where we spent a few pleasant days after the Chateau Thierry drive, and we stopped for a while at Domblain the station at which we detrained on that former occasion.

Our last stop tonight was Neuf chateau where we scrambled out and got into the coffee line at the Red cross canteen.

MAR. 7

This morning we woke at Kurthaus having crossed the line last night. We no longer can see the PG's working in parties along the route but see the square heads in a semi-free state in their own country.[4]

At Trier we again stopped for coffee and since the fourth division fellows got off here for good we changed into a better coach to finish our journey in.

We came into Coblenz at about one o'cloc. Here we lined up for mess and waited for the trucks which were to take us back to the outfit.

We started at 2:30 but the orders now do not permit fast running and our pace was slow. Going through the streets of Coblenz the men aroused some commotion by yelling at the MP's and asking them "who won the war?"

We sometimes think that the Yanks do not show their authority in Germany enough, that we do not impress the Huns with our strength but today I have come to a different conclusion for over the fortress of Ehrenbreitstein, on the Rhein a huge American flag floated. It simply dominated the surrounding country and could not but fail to impress upon every one that we are complete masters of this land which we have occupied.

An observation balloon was up at a very high altitude near the fortress, while an areoplane flew over the city. Then too as we came through one town it was time for retreat and the troops were assembling. That is a ceremony which appears beautiful to the soldier as well as to the layman, for when "To the colors" are played the companies came to parade rest. Then as "The Star Spangled Banner" is played the men in ranks come to present arms while the officers salute. This takes place while the flag is lowered.

The Rhine now accomodates more commerce than it did when we came some of them fly the American flag. An interesting sight to me is the tug towing up a string of three or four barges. It seems incredible that such a little ship can pull such a bunch of heavily laden barges.

We reached Neuenahr at five and made directly for the kitchen.

Seems kinda good to get back to the outfit after all, come to think of it this was the only time I had been away from the battery more than a day since leaving Fort Harrison Sept. 7, 1917.

12 Home

The war over, the Yanks wanted to go home, but had to await the availability of transportation. Most of the soldiers of the American Expeditionary Forces (AEF) did not get back until April or May. In the interim they were bored and half mutinous over the busywork the officers arranged. Let it be said that the officers had little choice in the matter, for Gen. John J. Pershing told his commanders to keep the men busy and out of mischief. The winter thus passed. Compared with British troops sent to such places as the Middle East and India or Australians with no possibility of home leaves, the Americans were better off, considering that most of the divisions came over in the spring and summer of 1918. But the two six-month overseas stripes that made Elmer Sherwood feel superior to a general in the United States weighed heavily upon members of the 150th Field Artillery Regiment, and they wanted to go home.

MAR. 8 Saturday-morning inspection and review of regt by Lt. Col Heath. This review business is a daily occurence since the Lt. Col assumed command during the Colonels sickness and the boys resent so much of it especially since the commander is a bird from SOS who has never seen service.[1] It is rather funny to see the change of sentiment toward [Robert H.] Tyndall. Everybody used to cuss him but now we want him to get well so that he can come back to the outfit.

MAR. 9 Sunday stood only formations reville and retreat, so I wrote some letters, making up for lost time. Of the letters I was especially glad to answer the one from Dad saying the manuscript for R-H [*Rainbow Hoosier*] had been received and that B.T. [Booth Tarkington] had agreed to write the foreword.

MAR. 10 We stood three rigid inspections today. They are surely putting us thru the mill in preparation for the review of div. by Pershing which is set for Sunday.

MAR. 11

Ordinary routine day. Drill, review, inspection.

MAR. 12

On range all day; each man firing fifteen rounds at 200 yd and ten rounds at 300 yd. It was great sport and I made a better score at 300 than at 200; in fact was quite a bit above average; but I have never had enough practice to shoot really well.

MAR. 13

Review before Lt. Col and usual inspections in morning. I received permission to visit Col Tyndall at the hospital in afternoon so took manuscript for RH with me and went to his room. He was reclining on a couch and looks very weak and pale but he assured me that he felt much better than since taken sick and expects to put his uniform on tomorrow. I read him several chapters of the mms. and he would interrupt whenever he had a suggestion or criticism in this way I received much valuable information and help. An interesting thing to me was his criticism of the use of the words Pershing's crusaders he said American crusaders was better because Pershing had not proven out. That he was simply a victim or rather beneficiary of circumstances, politics, and West Pointism. I am going back tomorrow to finish the reading and then hope to get a signed statement from him concerning it.[2]

MAR. 14

I am cpl of guard today so do not have to drill and am spending some time in writing. Received letter from Pearl today in which she said the folks had received all the pictures I had sent from Germany. I notice in the Citizen that the home town will probably get a 80,000 federal bldg and a 75,000 high school bldg this year.

MAR. 15

Regimental review in forenoon. Afternoon spent in cleaning equipment and in getting ready for the big inspection.

MAR. 16

Revillee 5:30 had breakfast and at 7:00 a prelimenary inspection. At 8:00 left Neuenahr hiking to great field on banks of Rhine near Raemagen in route order, arriving at 12:00. We were on the field standing in one spot for five hours, every rank of the entire division being inspected by Gen. Pershing. Then we passed in review before him. Lastly listening to a speech from the C in C in which he praised the division and the individuals composing it. We were worn out when we left the field at 6 pm and started our hike homeward but luckily the four trucks of the battery met us on the road and we all piled in reaching our billets at about seven.[3]

MAR. **17**	At noon the battery left town with the entire motor equipment tractors pulling guns and caissons, trucks with kitchen behind. We certainly were a different looking outfit today than when equipped with horses and we made some speed too. I was on the

truck hauling the kitchen, and as luck would have it the Col. said our kitchen needed more cleaning so when we came to the part of the road where we were to await the inspectors I had to get a detail of the fellows to clean it up. It started raining and we waited until after five, when attention was blown and Pershing with his entourage passed by in a flock of motor cars. The inspection was over that quick and we turned around as quick as we could and were off. The road looked just as if it were on the front during a battle, for all the outfits of the division were jamming the road. The 149 FA and 151 F.A. still have the horses and they were all groomed up and looking slick. 150 M.G. batallion had some fine looking horses and supply train had some fine mules.[4]

It seemed strange to see the old guns pulled by tractors and we did whiz in the trucks getting in at about 6:30 after mess we were ready for bed and thank goodness there are no more inspections for awhile.

MAR. **18**	Rained all day and we didn't have many formations. Last night Lt. Paul learned of his promotion to 1st. lieut. Capt Barbour to major and Lt. Bennet to Capt. I hear them celebrating in the next room now.

Rene La Febre; our cook and a Belgain, came back to the outfit today after a visit to his home near Burges. He was telling me about the trip and he said "Poy I got one helluva goot time." but he said that three days after reaching home which he hadn't seen for six years he got homesick for the battery. ["]Poy vat vill ve do venn ve get oudt of de armee" he says. He said he felt so happy when he came back to see all of us. But he says that he is going back to Belgium next winter to get his sweetheart. He tried to marry her while there this time but he had no american papers.

He told about the things his family had suffered during the occupation by the Boche. A typical instance was of his sister, while she was making the Ger lieuts bed (billeted in their home) he grabbed her; but she struck him squarely in the face and knocked him out. Next day she was arrested and sent to jail where she slept on a bench while confined there four days. But she didn't mind the jail sentence. René says his 16 year old cousin has a German baby and naturally feels very badly about the fact. Also his uncle's wife. The uncle was in the Belgian army.

Rene says his father is wise and told how he hid their cow in the celler but now they can't get it out. He told about how the Huns collected food. For each hen the housewife had to turn over to the Germans two eggs per week. The old priest had four hens and a rooster. He turned over the eight eggs per week but was fined each time because he didn't produce two a week for the rooster.

Rene told of one of his old pals who refused to dig trenches for the Huns. He ran away and stayed for a year and a half when he visited his home again. The soldiers heard him upstairs in the garret and went after him but he jumped from a window and then made for a river in rear of the house. He swam across and as he came out on the opposite shore two bullets struck him in the back and two guards went after him. He fought them until he died.

The father said that often a Belgian was killed because he walked the street without a permit (killed on grounds he was a spy). He said all the good Germans were dead. Meaning there wasn't such a thing as a good German, of course. They almost lived entirely off food furnished by the American relief commission he said. Even then the Huns stole much of it.

Belgium now is a changed place however. They dance all night and day. René says the people are as crazy as he is. He visited Brussels also. When going down he met his brother who is in the Belgian army. Rene says he had on medals and fine uniform and all, to make up Rene said, all that Rene lacked in being a soldier.

MAR. 19

Turned in jerkins and extra trousers today and have left only what we can easily carry on our backs.

One of the fellows was talking to an ex-German Soldaten who had been wounded July 14 in Champagne by a Alabamans bullet. He said they knew the Rainbow div. was there and that we sure gave them an awful set back. They thot the French and British were good soldiers but the Americans were best. Then he was switched to Chau. Thierry front and got the surprise of his life when he found that 42d was again there. this time doing the driving itself and doing it up brown.

MAR. 20

Fultz and I were on a day pass to the casino, so we spent the day over there going to movies and hearing the band etc and had a very enjoyable day of it.

I went to Lt. O'niels room and got list of casualties of the regiment. which by the way are the heaviest of the brigade.

MAR. 21 | Major Barbour called me up this morning and gave me a stack of orders, memorandums etc to classify and arrange chronologically so I did that most of the day. In doing so I ran across some interesting data for these orders are from Lorraine days to the present time. We got a shot in the arm for para typhoid. It was a dose five times the common injection and it makes ones arm sore.

MAR. 22 | Packed instruments and turned in all fire arms.

In evening Halli and I attended masked ball at casino. I had on a bell hop uniform and he was dressed as a girl—a good looking one too. The ball was a success and many gorgeous costumes were worn.

Got rid of last of our horses today. They were the cast offs of the lot and were sold at auction near Ahrweiler. The surprising part of it was that they brought average (8,500 marks—4,250 francs or $800) a team.

MAR. 23 | Only innovation of day was rolling of packs (practice for moving day[)] also had a field inspection and check up on equipment. Funny thing was that we got razors and soap issued—never happened during the war.

MAR. 24 | On guard last night and today. One post is at arcade where our equipment is stored. It will all be moved in the morning.

Some of the men took all of our guns and tractors up the Rhine where they turned them in. So we are now practically rid of everything except what we carry on our backs.

Tonight at about eleven I went down to the little park on the main street armed with a hammer and screw driver to get the metal Kaiser head on the statue there. At first I had to wait because the street lights were on and a good many people were passing. Then the lights went out and things grew quiet and I began. The metallic sound of hammering on the iron head—rang thru the night atmosphere and I was afraid some one would hear me and investigate, but they didn't bother so I went ahead deadening the sound by holding my hand over it, and finally got it off.

These damn Dutch claim that they dont like the Kaiser etc and some of them mean it but if he were to come back here after we leave I believe the fools would lick his boots again.

MAR. 25 | Have received letters from Guido, Aunt Ada and the folks Grandma wrote from New Symerna saying that she was anxious for me to get back since I had been gone so long but she added "Grandpa was away three years remember."

Six-inch guns of the 150th Field Artillery, stored in large covered court containing the "Crosser Sprudel," Neuenahr (Bad Neuenahr-Ahrweiler), Germany.

By the papers I note that the peace conference is as dilatory as ever and haven't settled anything yet. We want to get home but if they will let us go on to Berlin I know all the fellows would want to stay and see it through and settled right. Routine day.

MAR.
26

Rained all day and everything is sloppy and for a wonder we didn't do much except roll packs to select the one best suited to our future needs. Since material and horses are gone we have it rather easy not even a rifle or pistol to clean is fine.

MAR.
27

We got our usual weekly bath this morning. Everybody is anxious to keep clean for no one with cooties will be allowed to leave for U.S. Same applies to venereal cases. Glad I have no occasion to worry.

Battery elected four delegates to Rainbow division convention to be held at Neuenahr tomorrow they were. Lt. Paul. 1st Sgt Bowers, Sgt. Island and self. It made me feel good to be elected unanimously showing me that I do have every fellow for a friend. In evening I boarded a train and went to Raemagen where 165 Inf. (New York) is stationed to attend caucus of enlisted men. We got news that the higher officers were going to railroad things so wanted to make an effort for the bucks. We planned our opposition and finally (1 a.m) I was selected to nominated Maj Hughes for chairman of convention—because he is a square of man and not a party to the clique. I rode home in an ambulance and got to bed at 3:30 a.m. rising of course at 6:30.

**MAR.
28** Delegates of 150 F.A. met at 8:00 and decided upon a course of action in convention before going to casino. The casino was arranged according to plan by organizations and the signs standing by seats of different unit delegates gave it the appearance of a big political convention. Temperory chairman Col. Screws opened the meeting and called for nominations for permanent chairman and I was on my feet with a Mr. Chairman a couple of seconds later another delegate was up and the chair recognized him instead. He made the motion that the temperory chairman be made perm. chair. while I nomin Hughes. But he had benefit of first vote and won over Hughes. So we were beaten at the start. Screws has a personality and kept the convention laughing and beautifully railroaded things but we got in some good and desirable points in the constitution at that. Colonel Hough, 166 INF elected pres. Col. Riley 149 FA V.P. Corp Manning 2 V.P. Lt. Col.____ 3 V.P. Col. Leach Treas. Maj _____ Historian and Sgt. Maj Brown Sec. Father Duffy Chaplain. Washington DC. was voted headquarters of the "Rainbow Division Veterans" and Birmingham, Ala. obtained convention for 1920. Date July 15-16-17 Selected because our greatest battle in Champagne was on 15th July. Our meals were served in Kurhaus Restaurant and in evening a good show was produced (army talent) for us. Everybody departed with a feeling that a good work had been accomplished.

**MAR.
29** Made full packs this morning and then hiked with them on our backs the object being to toughen us again for some road work which we will have on our journey to Brest.

**MAR.
30** Rolled packs and had inventory in field while our stuff was exposed it began snowing and has continued all day. This evening my pal Sgt Ingram came in and in course of time argued me into shaving off my wonderfully cultivated moustache. Attended farewell Rainbow service at casino tonight. 151 band and quartet were on program and Father Duffy of N.Y. spoke. He is a "regular guy" and related our past experiences and future aims, hoping that we would go home to accomplish things instead of acting like heroes all our lives.

When we returned from the service I found Vernon Herbert in my room. He has been with the Marines from Chau Thierry through whole war and once at Exermont we came close to each other without knowing it at the time.

MAR. 31 | I got the day off to entertain Vernon so we spent the morning in talking over old times in Linton—B.K.R.T. [?] etc, and learned that Ira Shiffen is the only member who has died. He was killed in action. We had dinner at Restaurant and I think he has had a pretty good time—poor fellow there is no telling when he will get home as he is in the regulars and may stay a year. At Battery delegates to Indiana chapter of Rainbow Division Veterans were elected and I was informed that I was one of the twenty also that I am to run for Historian.

APR. 1 | Vernon went back to his outfit this morning as his pass was only a short one—But we had a good visit even tho short. Entire regiment passed in review before Gen. [George C.] Gatley this morning. Then the gen decorated the regimental standard with red streamers bearing names of battles in which we had participated. Perry came back after three weeks on journey to Is-Sur-Tille. [Sherwood added:] Gatley is father of Ann Harding; movie star.

APR. 2 | Regular drill and calisthenics. Saw a good movie at casino.

APR. 3 | Regular drill and calisthenics. Lined up in order in which we get on boat. Final physical inspection.

APR. 4 | At check inspection today Col. Tyndall said that it was his opinion that B battery is the best Battery in the regiment which of course made us proud of the old outfit.

APR. 5 | Convention convened at 10:30 this morning and I happened to be on committee on constitution and worked on it in morning. In afternoon officers were elected Hon Pres. Archy Pres. Prather. V.P. Taylor and two DSC men. T Glossbrenner, S. Huber Hist. Lt. O'niel. 1st conv. Indianapolis.

APR. 6

Received reserve rations and learn that we leave Neuenahr day after tomorrow. Service held in memory of rgt. dead.

APR. 8

Tues. Moving day. Reville as usual this morning 6:30 and after breakfast four men from each battery and cooks went to Rgt headquarters which we left via trucks at 8:00 a.m. arriving at Sinzig half an hour later. We went to town major's office and obtained our billeting list. This time our battery got the town theater for a bedroom. After leaving our packs in the theater we went down to a pioneer kitchen for the noon meal which consisted of slum and beans Wherever soldier eat kids and often the men and women (German) gather with pans to get the leavings which they take home for their own consumption. At this time the poor class is rather hard up for food but they will be alright after the approaching harvests.

After dinner we went to the bridge and awaited the trucks which carried the battery packs. These we directed to the opera house. The battery left Neuenahr at 2:00 hiking to Sinzig in two hours.

After supper at the battery kitchen Ingram and I took a walk about the old town. Remains of the ancient walls are still standing and many of the houses of the town are old. The side of the town toward the Rhine is filled with industrial plants. The main industry along the Rhine is wine making. I suppose Rheinwein is of course famous ranking with Champagne in the better brands most fellows prefer the latter though.

The latest name applied to troops of the third army is "Amaroc" being a combination of the first syllables of the American army of Occupation. I do not believe that it will become so widely known however as "Yanks" under which name we served throughout the war.

APR. 9

Slept pretty well on the floor last night. After breakfast we rolled rolls and marched to the railway station 10:30 where we remained until 1:00 when the train pulled out.

Of course we are all happy to be on the way. We were all d____ anxious to come over and do our bit and are all equally d____ anxious to get home after the bit has been done. But no one is hilarious, in fact we can scarcely realize that it is true. A correspondent speaking of the Rainbow division called it "blasé" and I believe he was right for tho something new might be sprung on us nothing could surprise us. So we take this going home as a part of the same game. We do appreciate our fortune however as we pass thru the towns and villages and see the cluster of homesick American soldiers staring at us and perhaps waving us a good bye backed by a sickly grin. So long as the Yanks were fighting there was no time for homesickness but this killing time breeds the disease so when in Neuenahr the best place in the A of O territory we were not as satisfied as on the front doing battle. At that former time too we never knew what would happen next but on this trip we know just what to expect which also takes away some of the interest.

As we go along we always point out anything American for instance "There's an American locomotive. Thats an American automobile etc. It is hard to imagine that in a month this will all change until we note not things that are American but things that are foreign, however I know our opinion that what is American, generally speaking, is best, will not change notwithstanding the proverb familiarity breeds contempt."

In passing through Andernach we saw again the ancient town walls and gates which are still standing in a fine state of preservation. On the plain on left bank of Rhine near the town are many big brick plants and concrete factories. They seem to be running full force now. In the last few months work has picked up wonderfully in Rheinland.

The major refused to allow us to put up our banners which read "Homeward bound to Indiana" and from "Hell to Heaven," saying that it was unmilitary, such is the narrow view of such men.

Approaching Coblenz an areoplane flew over the train. American flags are prominent all thru the occupied territory but the greatest one flies over the fortress of Ehrenbreitstein opposite Coblenz. An observation bal-

Troops passing through the victory arch on Meridian Street, Welcome Home Day Parade, Indianapolis, 1919. In May 1919 Indianapolis welcomed the state's fighting men back home.

loon was also up giving a picture of the domination of democracy hitherto unparalleled in history. Old glory certainly does hold the greatest position in her history. It is a sign of justice and hope backed up by righteous force.

In the underground passage of the fortress the Americans found vast stores of ammunition and equipment and for months they have been blowing them up.

From Coblenz our route lay thru the valley of the Moselle. The river of course is not so large as the Rhine but the valley appeared just as beautiful to me as that of the Rhine. The Rhine is famous for its castles but I saw only a few of them between Coblenz and Cologne while in our days journey through the Moselle valley I saw scores of them, ruined and restored. Many built on the most inaccessable heights. At Coburn there are terraced vineyards upon the hills just as great as those in the Rhine valley a quaint old village lies on the river bank here, with houses the architecture of which dates to medieval times. Upon the overshadowing hill above the village is a fine old castle with part of its walls still standing. At Gondorf and Cattenour a wonderful and big old castle crowned the largest hill on the opposite bank of the river. It was a fortress which had also the advantage of being pleasing to the eye. Its points of defense were two towers and the living apartments were no doubt located in the part of the castle between the towers, which had been covered outside by growing vines. At Cachever was another fine example of a castle.

It was dark when we reached Trèves (Trier) so we spread our blankets on the floor of the car, softened by the mattresses and prepared for sleeping. But the car, being crowded our trains averaged between 40 and 58 men to the car some horseplay was bound to be given vent to. After a few scuffles we settled down but one fellow in the opposite end of the car insisted upon lighting a candle desiring to read. There was a roll of paper near me and with careful aim I imitated a grenade thrower and let go, the missel making a fine hit—target and the fellow didn't have nerve to light another.

APR. 10 | We passed thru Metz at 2:30 this morning the trainman said; but when we awoke we had reached Etain a destroyed village. We took a siding and had breakfast served. The fields about were torn by many shell holes—so we have again entered the land which is a scar upon the face of fair France a scar which will take hundreds of years to heal.

As we continued our journey the land became more and more torn indeed every one wondered how the engineers had been able to reconstruct this rail road bed thru some of these places. This old battle ground—perhaps greatest of the war (before Verdun) is now strangely quiet—where once the guns belched forth their messages of death and brave heroes died by thousands and hundreds of thousands—now it is desolate only once in a while we see a few American soldiers working sometimes with gas masks on, for gas lurks in many places even now.

A soldier can not realize fully that it is all over. We had become used to war fare—nothing surprised us and even now we could go back to battle without wondering a great deal. But it is fine that it is over and the victory is ours. Not because thru it America is proven to be the mightiest of all nations but because she is now recognized as the best. Old glory stands for righteousness throughout the world today. It was a terrible price but it was worth it.

At 9:00 am after coming thru the territory the hills of which had been the stumbling block of the Boche and the saving defense of the Allies and after journeying through the famous Verdun tunnel which also leads under the town itself we came to Verdun.

They shall not pass was the shibboleth here and they didn't pass altho the Huns had come close and had lain the town waste. Trenches, bomb and shell holes have mutilated the old town; but it is not so completely destroyed as scores of other towns we have journeyed thru.

An American engineer whose station is Verdun came to our train inquiring for me. He is from Linton and knew that I was with this outfit so he had kept looking for me. After talking about people and the old town. He spoke of Verdun saying that a few of the inhabitants were now returning here to live. I told him that the town was not so large as I had expected and not so completely destroyed; but he said it was the worst pile of debris he had ever lived in. The cathedral of Verdun is a massive structure having two main towers. It is on a flat topped hill and dominates the town; behind it south lies the Meuse valley, so it can easily be seen why Verdun was the key so greatly desired by both sides.

We journeyed down the valley to St. Mihil the town famous in American history because our drive in September took its name from it, tho practically no fighting was done in the town itself. It is one of the freaks of history that towns give their names to great operations when the heavy fighting has been done at another point viz. Chau. Thierry. St. Mihil also is in a valley and is protected by the hills to the N. and E. The main part of the town is on the E bank of the Meuse.

Thru Bar-Le-Duc, Revigny and Sermaize we came to Vitry-Le-Francois. The last town is the one at which our battery detrained in July when going to the Champagne front and that battle of the 14th and 15th where the fate of the German army was sealed. The stopping of the [?] German drive in Champagne was of the same importance to the Allies in this war as the battle of Gettysburg was to the Union forces in the Civil War.

In night passed Sommesous, Seganne, Coulommiers (not far from Chau Thierry), Versailles. Eiffel tower is about the only thing in Paris we can see but we passed within a good view of the great palace where the treaty of peace will be signed.

Sille-le-Guillaume (Suppe) polish H.Q. we passed in evening. Troops ready to go to Poland.

It was nightfall when we reached Boissy.

APR.
11

This morning we reached Versailles. The next city of importance on the route was Chartres. The cathedral of Chartres is one of the finest in France, a Gothic structure superior to Notre Dame I believe.

Le Mans was the next important city. Here is one of the centers of A.E.F. activities, and the Americans have a great camp near it. The town is one of the old style resembling Rennes. The latter city we passed at ab[o]ut 2:30 a.m.

APR.
12

Rain. Breton lands greet our view this morning. The quaint old land patched into fragments by hedge rows, brush rows, and dirt banks. Newer wire fences but these other methods of fencing are used notwithstanding the fact that a great deal of valuable space is lost by the ancient method.

We pass over Morlaix. It is a picturesque old town in the valley. From the train we look down upon its roofs. Now we are in the valley of Elorn which flows into Brest harbor. It is now low tide and many people are out on the banks gathering musseles. Fishing villages now dot our route sail boats are numerous. Old women with white caps wooden shoes and sometimes pantaloons instead of the black petticoats are to be seen everywhere.

At eleven thirty our train pulled into Brest, detrained and lined up for mess. The regiment was fed in less than an hour because of the system used a bunch of coons did the cooking and serving. The line of soldiers passed the counters where they dished food passed on to lines of tables at which they stood and ate.

After the meal we swung on our packs for the up hill hike to Camp Pontanezen about three miles distant. It was a tough hike and we were all in when we reached our camp at the extreme end of the larger camp. We have tents with wooden floors and small stoves. The camp is not so bad as I expected since all the talk about conditions here. Of course it is muddy because it rains almost every day. The camp paper put out a big laudetory article on the division in this evenings edition.

APR.
13

Rain. Entire bat. took bath this morning. Bath scientific as meals (3 minute) turn out clean men as fast as Ford automobiles.

APR.
14

Rain. Each day each outfit furnishes details to load coal at docks etc. Secy of War [Newton D.] baker has arrived on USS Leviathan with ambassador [Henry] White. This is the ship we take back.

The div. was honored today at a ceremony in public square of Brest. Vice-Admiral Moreau, governor of Brest inspected guard of honor and presented the cravat of a commander of the Legion of Honour on General [George W.] Read, who is new div. commander. I understand that the gen has never seen any of this war on the fighting front—had some job in S.O.S. It is a shame to give him this honor when [Charles T.] Menoher led us through the fighting, but c'est la Guerre. Crosses of the Legion were conferred on other officers.

The admiral read a letter written in M. [Georges] Clemenceau's own hand, paying eloquent tribute to the services of the division.

APR.
15

Rain. Carried our reserve rations to warehouse today. Practically all ruined of course by journey from Germany. A great waste of money and good example of army red tape. We carried these rations upon our backs for miles and there was no need of them but—. Rain of course.

APR.
16

Medical inspection this afternoon and pay day. Pay in American money. One can get the best idea of how long we have been gone from the Land of the Free by the fact that we never saw some of this model currency before.

At midnight we took our packs to inspection bldg where officers inspected them. More unnecessary red tape.

APR.
17

Rain. After breakfast we set out on the hike to port at 7 am. The hike was a little better going than coming because it was largely down hill. We got into the big shelters at the wharf where we were held up for the night because the sea was too rough to load. We got cots into the place and rested fine.

APR.
18

Rain. Loaded at about nine our ferry boat looked like a speck beside the Leviathan. We walked up the gang plank from the midget to the monster and taken to our compartments.

This ship is the largest in world.
Standard speed—16 knots
Emergency speed—23 knots
Speed being made on this trip—20 knots
length—950 feet
Beam—100 feet

Displacement—68,000 tons
Keel to top of mast—297 feet
Horsepower—65,000
Engines—4 turbine
Decks—13, besides bridge
Crew—2,083
three stacks including dummy

Marsh and I travelled the boat from top to bottom. It is not only big
but magnificent. It rocks very little and is fitted out like a great hotel.
Swimming pool is a big tile one. Dining room is big and fine. Rest rooms
libraries etc—elevators.

Left Brest 5 p.m. while band played Home, sweet Home and Smiles.—
Every body happy? hell yes. The Aquitania sister ship of Lusitania sailor
told us, led us out of Brest, a port filled with ships flying the American flag.
Some French battlships there too.

This sure is the day of days we are just as anxious to go home as we
were to come across. It has been a great experience and of course a necessary task but we hope it wont have to be repeated. The bunks are more
comfortable and less crowded than on the Lincoln.[5] [Sherwood added:]
We stayed on deck until land disappeared.

APR.
—
19 I am on a baggage detail. We are taking baggage to staterooms
etc. among baggage handled was some for Ambassador Sharp
who has resigned position to White, Maj Gen G. W. Read Maj
Gen S. D. Sturgis of 80th div; Brig Gen Douglass MacArthur 84
Brigade, Ex secty Treas O. T. Crosby Ex-postmaster gen Hitchcock and
three congressmen.

Army units on board:

149th F. A.	Casual details St. Aignan detach.
150th F. A.	Cas. Co. 704
166th Inf	Brest cas. det.
168th Inf	sick and wounded #184 to #192
117 gas train	
117 T.H. and MP	Total 11505 officers and men[6]
42 div Hq troop	
Hq det. 84 Brigade	
at 8:00 am	Brest 281 mi
	New York 2878 mi

The sad sight on ship are the one legged men over two hundred of
them. The war never will be over for them but they are much better off
than the "nuts" of whom there are a number in a caged compartments.

IHS, Bass Photo Company Collection, 66377

Court of Allies, Welcome Home Day Parade, Indianapolis, 1919.

Shell shock nervousness etc have contributed to make them lose their minds.

The food aboard is fine tho only two meals a day. Same system in great dining hall as in the camps.

APR.
20

Easter sunday—excellent turkey dinner. In evening picture show in dining room.

APR.
21

"A sweet young thing" member of one of the parties aboard, was heard to remark yesterday that she would like to see the cattle feed. So this morning every doughboy aboard has heard of it and tho none of us can help but feel insulted there are many jokes about it, for instance as we were going to mess this morning the mooing of cows was initiated. Of course the girl should be spanked or if too old punished in another way for such a brainless and unpatriotic expression. It would not have been resented had a soldier said it, for of course the way we feed isn't much different than the way animals are fed. But having fought for such as her we deserve more than sneers. However we have learned much about snobbishness and caste since going to war.

In the crowds packed in the mess hall many men with an arm or a leg gone are to be seen. Any reasonable person would think that a bed in a stateroom, such as the officers have, would be nothing too much to give them; but they have the same uncomfortable canvas bunks as we.

No doubt the American soldier will be a force in American life and politics. We should be and the principle which we now desire to uphold is equality. I saw a picture in "Life" yesterday of an Irish laborer in shirt sleeves riding home from work in an automobile. That is funny now but I hope that it is not a joke long because the man who works hard thru the day deserves a motor car as much as any one in the world. High wages are right, if a man is a worker he deserves a better living than he has had in the past. Of course no one should be paid for work he doesnt do. A good worker is a rare find so a man should be paid in proportion to what he accomplishes The piece work system is right. And high wages for labor is right. We cannot do away with snobbishness but we can change the money status upon which the American caste system is built and the political system is made corrupt.

The army has been a frightful example to us of the least work getting the highest reward of favoritism, money value, caste and snobbishness. It hasn't been wholly bad of course but we have learned that we don't want the same system in the govt. of the nation.[7]

The A.L.A. has distributed a bunch of magazines so we have plenty to read.[8] Band concerts are a regular event and movies are given in the big mess hall, so our time is passed fairly pleasantly.

APR. 22 | I met the correspondent of Cleveland Ledger on deck this morning and during the conversation told him that I had been studying journalism when I joined the army. He told me that the journalistic profession was the lowest paid in the world and tho he had gotten farther than the average newspaper man he was sorry he had followed it. I told him that I hadn't been able to sell my book and he said that that was nothing for he had been refused by the publishers and he had all kinds of material. He said that Floyd Gibbons was the only correspondent who had gotten away with a book.[9] This whole experience has taught me a few things about air castles. I realize that I have taken myself at least, too seriously and if I can get a moderate success in the metropolis of Linton I will be doing well.

Attended show in dining room tonight, given by members of Rainbow Div. and enjoyed it. The participants are planning to tour in the states and I believe they will make good. It is quite an experience to attend a show in such a large room while speeding on thru the ocean. The Leviathan is so large that there is very little rocking so one can imagine that he is in a theater on land, such is the development of the Modern world.

IHS, Bass Photo Company Collection, 66355F

Wounded soldiers riding through the Court of Allies in the Welcome Home Day Parade, Indianapolis, 1919.

APR.
23

I have spent most of the day on deck. This morning the sea was rather rough and the spray was so thick that it resembled rain, but the sun has been summer bright.

Spent day mainly in reading "A Yankee at the Court of King Arthur" by Mark Twain, enjoyed it as much as any of his work I ever read.

Sent wireless home "Not run over by street car. Land tomorrow." Mom will know what first sentence means I believe, for whenever I ever went away from home she would warn me not to get run over by the street cars and when I left for France she told me the same thing.

APR.
24

There have been some prizefights on board this ship during the voyage but today's matches were the best. The sailors generally are in better condition than soldiers but there are some fine matches.

Sea is more rough today than it has been so far and while the mountainous waves pile up and smash against the ships side with a roar like that of distant artillery the old boat goes serenely on with little rocking.

APR.
25

Morning spent in rolling packs and policing up in bunk rooms.
Passed a light or patrol boat and it was rocking in the rough sea so that we could see only half of it at a time.
Drew into port at five and came in with tide, disembarking at about 7 p.m.[10] While waiting for the ferry at Hoboken the relief organizations served us pie.

After ferrying across the Hudson we entrained and journeyed to Camp Merritt N.J. which we reached 2 a.m.

APR.
26

Went thru decootizing process today.

APR.
27

Bought a flock of newspapers and spent day in reading them. Ich and I went to Liberty Theater in evening.

APR.
28

Went to N.Y. in evening, stopping at Beta Club. Saw (Monte Cristo Jr.) Wintergarden—fair.

APR.
29

Slept late. Saw Yanks vs. Athletics game afternoon and "Tumble in" night.

APR.
30

Returned to camp this morning [—] Attended K.C. dance and had a good time.

MAY
1

Papers tell of strikes all over country today even Linton got on the N.Y. newspapers fronts with a riot. Loafed around today.

IHS, Bass Photo Company Collection, 50772F

Soldiers disembarking from train, Indianapolis, 1919. Sherwood's father came to the train to welcome him home.

MAY
2

Went in to N.Y. tonight and visited Universal offices with Fink, who introduced me to Mr. Schintzer gen mgr distrib. Then had dinner at his home and saw movie in eve.

MAY
3

Time drug out today so in evening I went to Patterson to see the little girl whom I met at the K.C. dance and spent a pleasant evening.

MAY
4

I got ambitious today and washed my belt and haversack besides under clothing.
  Visited with Allie and wife for a while this afternoon.

MAY
5

Entrained at 1:30 Camp Merritt in tourist cars—very swell after the box car varieties we are used to.
  Everett Watkins of Star took my book and read it, expressing a high regard for it and asking for a copy which he can review at length in the paper.[11]
Ingram and I are bunkies on a lower.

Col. Robert H. Tyndall leading Rainbow Division in Welcome Home Day Parade, Indianapolis, 1919. The returning soldiers were welcomed by cheering throngs as they passed in review.

MAY
——
6

The train is receiving a constant ovation from the people all along the route. I never saw so many pretty girls before as line the station platforms.

At noon we stopped in Lima Ohio and paraded more for exercise than show I presume. When we reached Cleveland we stopped at 105 st. station for breakfast so I ran into the station and called Ethel. She was lucky in getting a neighbor to drive her down in a jiffy. She didnt wait for the machine to stop but jumped out into my arms with a bang, and of course cried as for me I couldn't say anything for a while. After a half hour the train moved on.

Tonight the trains are in the yards at Tipton.

MAY
——
7

This morning while washing, before the train had started Dad came of course words couldn't express the joy of either of us. Soon the train started toward Indianapolis, with cheering crowds at every station. We would hold our hands out the windows and touch the rows of hands extended toward us.

Upon arrival at Indianapolis we lined up and marched to Military park. It seemed as if all the whistles in the state had been turned loose.

Notes

CHAPTER ONE

1. The army did not have enough artillery pieces, light or heavy, to equip its field artillery regiments and relied upon French guns, available once the regiments reached France. There they were equipped with so-called French 75s, three-inch guns, and 155s, heavy artillery, the 150th receiving the latter.

2. Doroteo Arango, known as Pancho Villa, led a rebellion against the central government in Mexico City controlled by a rival and in 1916 raided Columbus, New Mexico, killing seventeen American citizens. President Woodrow Wilson called out the National Guard and sent Brig. Gen. John J. Pershing into Mexico with 6,600 troops in pursuit of the murderous Villa. The Indiana artillery battalion was among units sent to the border.

3. In army parlance the word police means simply assignment to duty, camp police being a cleanup detail. The top cutter was the first sergeant.

4. The game was poker or craps.

5. "You sure have a wide choice in New York. The Follies was real good—the prettiest scenic effects and coloring of scenery and costumes I ever saw. The songs were real good as was Bert Williams—otherwise nothing extraordinary. Doc Sherwood and I went together." William A. Seward to Edith Register, Sept. 13, Seward Papers, Forty-second Division survey, U.S. Army Military History Institute, Army War College, Carlisle Barracks, Pa.

6. Tulip was Sherwood's invention. Columbia City (present-day population 5,706) is northwest of Fort Wayne.

7. Secretary of War Newton D. Baker reviewed the troops and neither he nor the Rainbow's senior officers and military leaders in Washington (Major Generals Hugh L. Scott, Tasker H. Bliss, and John Biddle) sensed that such training was a waste of time. Marching 28,000 men up Garden City streets did nothing to prepare them for war. The Forty-second had not even come together as a unit until it assembled at Camp Mills. Officers and men needed time for field exercises. In the single largest battle of American troops during World War I, the Meuse-Argonne, involving 1.2 million men, with 26,000 deaths, division commanders and senior officers could not handle the large units and lost regiments and even brigades. Opportunity presented itself in the first days of the Meuse-Argonne, but commanders failed to avail themselves of it. As a result, the Germans brought in reinforcements and changed the tactical situation from one of movement to one of position—from

which the Americans escaped only in the battle's last days. The training of which Sherwood was so proud was useless. Close-order drill at Fort Harrison and marching around the dusty roads of Long Island was what a later generation described as counterproductive. It tired the men without purpose.

8. Sherwood's father was part owner of the *Linton Citizen*. Undated clipping, Sherwood Papers, Lilly Library, Indiana University, Bloomington, Ind. Phil Reyburn, "Letters from a World War I Soldier," *Indiana Military History Journal* 1 (Jan. 1972), 11–13, reprinted the diary of the voyage, but Reyburn's text differs in a few particulars from that in the *Citizen*.

9. According to a member of the 150th's headquarters company, Vernon E. Kniptash of Indianapolis: "I saw one fellow go to the mess room, get his mess, come out on deck to eat it, look at it, and get pale behind the gills, take his mess hurriedly to the garbage can, and a still more hasty manner make a beeline for the rail. When he snapped all that was possible, he put on a sheepish grin and reckoned as how he didn't enjoy either meal very much." E. Bruce Geelhoed, comp. and ed., "The Kniptash Diaries: 1917–1919" (unpublished manuscript, Ball State University, 1999), Oct. 20.

10. Nine out of ten sightings were in error, usually of debris from sunken ships. Sherwood seemed ambivalent about the danger of submarines, but Kniptash felt uneasy: "The captain said to expect a call at any time now. It all means we are right in the center of the war zone and all the chance in the world of taking a nice cold bath before morning." Ibid., Oct. 27.

11. The 150th's horses were not on the *Grant*. See chapter 2, n. 2.

12. The convoy comprised eight transports and four freighters.

13. Submariners could see the masts of a transport or freighter before lookouts from approaching ships could see the submarine, the latter being small with a low silhouette. Their tactic was to line up the masts, move to right or left at a ninety-degree angle, and wait for their quarry not far from its course. If the ship zigzagged, changing course erratically or according to a timetable if in convoy, the submarine could not attack with hope of success.

14. The people of France were known as "frogs" because they considered frog legs a delicacy.

15. The National Army was to be made up of draftees even though in practice the other two categories included draftees. Set in its ways, the army continued this fiction about its units. One of the distinctions awarded Regular Army divisions was to number them in a spelled-out manner, such as First Division, comprising the first ten divisions formed after the declaration of war.

16. Puts were puttees, a leather legging worn by officers; the men used wraparound cloth strips, a nuisance to put on and remove.

17. Corned willie was corned beef. The 150th did not begin to train until mid-November, to the annoyance of Colonel Tyndall: "We are all glad to get away and to our training as we have done nothing but build roads here, which is good practice for the men as they will have lots of digging to do later on." Robert Tyndall to [Dean Spellman Tyndall], Nov. 17, 1917, Robert H. Tyndall Collection, 1916–1943, M280, Indiana Historical Society, Indianapolis.

CHAPTER TWO

1. Although maintaining a diary was against army regulations, Sherwood and many other soldiers violated the rule, as evidenced by the many diaries deposited in the U.S. Army Military History Institute, Army War College, Carlisle Barracks, Pa.

2. The 40 x 8 refers to the French railroad cars so marked, for forty men or eight horses. When the 150th left camp its horses and mules had not yet arrived, and the men broke in new animals. A regimental detail left Fort Harrison with the animals for Newport News on October 1 and boarded the former German freighter *Bulgaria,* renamed *Hercules,* on January 16. During a storm at sea a hold sprang a leak and 241 animals drowned. A member of the detail, David H. Ramsay, helped drag out carcasses and threw them overboard. David H. Ramsay Diary, Feb. 6, Lilly Library, Indiana University, Bloomington; Paul L. Palmerton, ed., *Under the Rainbow: Battery F, 150th F.A.* (Indianapolis: The Battery, 1919), 5. When the horses finally caught up to the 150th the tales of the men who had brought them over were marvelous: "All the boys said they had a wicked trip across. Were 30 days getting across. Had a mutiny in the engine room. Had a German spy on board. Got lost from the convoy. Engines went bad. Floated around for 36 hours at the mercy of old man Neptune. Sprung a leak. Drowned 241 mules. Bailed water for four and $^1/_2$ days and finally landed in Ireland. Some trip, I claim. They were sure glad to see land. Carl said that, during that 36 hours they were drifting around hopelessly, he never saw as many soldiers reading the Bible at one time in all his life." E. Bruce Geelhoed, comp. and ed., "The Kniptash Diaries: 1917–1919" (unpublished manuscript, Ball State University, 1999), Mar. 2.

3. The word billet gained currency in World War I. Soldiers were assigned to barns and officers to rooms in houses.

4. The Africans were recruited from French colonies.

5. By wear he meant carry.

6. Another word often heard in 1917–18 was echelon. Sherwood here means regimental headquarters.

7. Emperor William II advised a contingent of troops going out to China during the Boxer Rebellion to oppose the Boxers as did the Huns of old, and thereby the American description.

8. HE stood for heavy explosive.

9. Snow was rumor. Because of the care necessary to keep horses in condition the prospect of trucks was exhilarating, but trucks did not arrive until January 1919.

CHAPTER THREE

1. A projector was a mortar.

2. Although balloons carrying people made their appearance in the eighteenth century and were used in the American Civil War, they did not come into their own until World War I, when they were used for observation across the front lines. Because German planes dominated the front, Allied observers were in constant trouble, as bullets would set their balloons on fire. The observers in the balloons wore parachutes and had to jump before the fiery mass of a balloon fell on the parachute, setting it afire and plunging the observer to his death. Moreover, balloons were precarious perches, as Col. George E. Leach of the 151st Field Artillery Regiment discovered: "At two P. M. I made my first balloon ascension and I never had to call on so much nerve before. I put on a fur lined suit and had the parachute strapped on me and climbed into a basket about four feet square and started up. The sensation was terrific, and when we got up about 2,000 feet the wind was blowing fourteen meters. When we started down the sensation was worse than going up, but I am glad the first time is over." George E. Leach, *War Diary* (Roanoke, Va.: National Association, Rainbow Division Veterans, 1962), 19–20 (Jan. 28, 1918).

3. Here was a very interesting situation. The Forty-second Division not merely was one of the first four divisions to go to France but it was enterprising in its tactics, in this instance willing to counter German gas shells. Later divisions hesitated to employ gas because of fear that clouds would drift back over their own lines, as happened with the Twenty-sixth Division on one occasion. In a memorandum of April 1, Brig. Gen. Charles H. McKinstry instructed his artillery colonels, including Tyndall, in discipline; that in case of attack the men at batteries should be thinned out as much as possible and relieved often; that they should take care to wear masks until there no longer was danger, especially from yperite, which was persistent; that the new oiled clothing was effective to prevent burns; and also application in contaminated areas of chloride of lime. Sixty-seventh F.A. Brig., G-3 memos, 1918, 32.15, box 25, Forty-second Division historical, entry 1241, RG 120, National Archives. On April 15 McKinstry told the colonels to retaliate for any attack, at least (underlined) 20 percent beyond whatever shells the Germans put over.

4. Band concerts took place at the front when weather permitted: "When the weather is cloudy or rainy so that the Germans have neither plane nor balloon observers, we try to have band concerts. Sometimes in the front line trenches, with the wind in the right direction, you can hear the German bands playing. At such times the firing is usually light." Leach, *War Diary*, 33–34 (Apr. 20, 1918). Bandsmen, one should add, were no luxury in the AEF, despite the fact that each regiment had a band, even the artillery regiments. During attacks the members of bands doubled as stretcher bearers and often were in intense danger.

5. Operations post.

6. The blank is in the diary, and Sherwood doubtless placed it there to avoid revealing his regiment's location, in case his diary was captured.

7. AWOL is absent without leave.

8. A fourgon was a two-wheeled wagon for carrying shells.

9. Battery E. Within the regiment each battery received a designation.

10. The purpose of a raid was to shake up defenders and obtain prisoners for questioning.

11. "The German plane had been far over our lines and was attacked by a French plane. The French airman got the German pilot with a machine gun bullet and then with incendiary bullets set the German plane on fire. The German pilot in spite of his wound tried to volplane to the German lines but the French airman headed him off. While the plane was still over one thousand feet in the air the Captain's observer jumped out and lit about one mile from where the plane did. He had all of his clothes burnt off and his body was so badly charred that one could never have recognized it. The pilot was in the plane, strapped in; and of course was simply burnt to death. When the plane came down it was in a mass of flames and when it lit it was mashed into a thousand pieces." Elmer Frank Straub, *A Sergeant's Diary in the World War: The Diary of an Enlisted Member of the 150th Field Artillery (Forty-Second [Rainbow] Division)* (Indianapolis: Indiana Historical Bureau, 1923), 87 (May 27, 1918). Straub was in Battery A.

CHAPTER FOUR

1. A heavy artillery regiment had three battalions, like infantry regiments, with batteries instead of the infantry's companies.

2. This was the German barrage and Allied countermeasures prior to the Germans' last offensive on July 15.

3. The attack was from the German salient. The 150th took part in interdiction fire, and the work of the guns was impressive: "Indeed, it was afterward stated that not since Verdun had there ever been so much artillery massed on one front, and never had the fire been of such volume and intensity. The sky, which was full of lowering clouds, was stained a dull, angry red by the flash and flare of thousands of guns, the atmosphere vibrated with the steady thunderous roar, a roar punctuated by the crash of shells bursting near and interlined with screeching wail of shells tearing their way through the upper strata of the air. It was the great symphony of war, and there was no cessation in artillery activity, no relief from the high tension and strain at which everyone worked, until late the following morning. Battery F ceased fire shortly before noon, and although firing was resumed in the afternoon and continued throughout the night and the following day, it was understood that we had broken the beast's 'paw.'" Paul L. Palmerton, ed., *Under the Rainbow: Battery F, 150th F.A.* (Indianapolis: The Battery, 1919), 17.

4. It was necessary to travel via Paris because the direct road to Lizy-sur-Ourcq was being shelled.

5. Oscar E. Bland, a Linton Republican, was born in Greene County, Indiana, in 1877 and graduated from Indiana University and Valparaiso University. A lawyer, he was elected to the Indiana legislature and in 1916 to the House of Representatives. He was a member of the Elks, Knights of Pythias, Eagles, Masons, Woodmen, and Sigma Nu.

CHAPTER FIVE

1. "Quite a few shells hit around us this morning, and this afternoon about 3 P.M., one hit near our caisson, which was on the road. It killed 3 horses and one man, Deans, and seriously injured Skidmore. Also slightly injured Dill and Biddle." Ervin M. Johannes Diary, July 28, 1918, Forty-second Division survey, U.S. Army Military History Institute, Army War College, Carlisle Barracks, Pa. Johannes was in Battery A, from Indianapolis, and knew Sherwood.

2. Gen. Erich Ludendorff described the British attack as his "black day," for he concluded that Germany was losing the war. British forces managed the advance with tanks, and the Germans were powerless to stop them.

3. Fellow members of the regiment were not as sanguine about the living arrangements, which to Sherwood's mind seem to have been tolerable if annoying. According to Vernon E. Kniptash, "Can't sleep in the daytime because of the flies and can't sleep at night because of shells" (Aug. 7). "One consolation is that the Germans are getting five [of] our shells for every one they put over. Just a steady roar of guns all the time. There are no dugouts and trenches and a fellow has to take his chances in the open" (Aug. 8). "Same filth, dirt, and shells and a hope for a relief soon. Our brigade is just about frazzled out and will have to be relieved shortly or something will bust. The strain and grind is too much" (Aug. 9). E. Bruce Geelhoed, comp. and ed., "The Kniptash Diaries, 1917–1919" (unpublished manuscript, Ball State University, 1999). According to Johannes, "About 11 P.M. last night shells hit very close to me. One hit a tree to the right of our tent about 25 ft. away. It cut the tree off about 10 ft. up and set the upper part right side of the trunk. Fragments fell all around here, and it wounded 3 of our men. One piece put a hole in the tent right by my head, and cut a cigarette box in two that was lying there." Johannes diary, Aug. 10.

4. It is difficult to keep the movements of the 150th in mind, and a brigade summary may help: "August 3rd to 11th. During this period the brigade was active

in breaking down enemy resistance north of the Vesle, and supporting our infantry which was establishing its lines across the river. The 150th F.A. during this period was active in counterbattery work against fugitive targets. On August 6th, after four hours' artillery preparation, the 4th Division advanced across the Vesle and reached the Rouen-Rheims road. From that time until August 11th the artillery was engaged in breaking up enemy counterattacks and against hostile strongpoints. On the night of August 10–11th the brigade was relieved by the 4th Brigade U.S. and that same night moved south across the Ourcq and went into bivouac in the vicinity of Moucheton Chateau." Brig. Gen. George C. Gatley to Maj. Gen. Charles T. Menoher, Sixty-seventh F.A. Brig., rept. of opns., July 24–Aug. 11, 1918, 33.6, box 36, Forty-second Division historical, entry 1241, RG 120, National Archives.

5. The army arranged mobile showers, after which the men received clean clothing. Attendants placed old clothing in a vat and boiled it to eliminate vermin.

6. At the beginning of their first offensive the Germans had employed the long-range gun that shelled Paris. It was a weapon of terror, dropping shells indiscriminately.

7. The car doubtless was a 40-and-8, suitable for forty men or eight horses.

8. Close-order drill was an easy way to move large bodies of troops, looked good in parades, and kept the men busy but carried few other benefits. Not long before the United States entered World War II, Gen. George C. Marshall told Col. J. Lawton Collins to eliminate it, which Collins did with enthusiasm. It found its way back and has continued to the present day.

9. RFC was Royal Flying Corps.

10. Sherwood's fraternity was Beta Theta Pi. A photograph of five Betas appeared in the *Indianapolis News*, June 2, 1918: Lee H. Hottell, Indianapolis; Sherwood; and George Reed, Cotton Rawles, and Allan Cauble, all of Bloomington. The group held a canteen representing a variant of a fraternity song, "We'll All Drink from the Same Canteen in Beta Theta Pi." Clipping, Elmer Sherwood Papers, Lilly Library, Indiana University, Bloomington, Ind.

CHAPTER SIX

1. It was a common complaint that representatives of the Salvation Army acted far better than officials of the YMCA, and after the war the YMCA defended itself by sponsoring Katherine Mayo's *That Damned "Y": A Record of Overseas Service* (Boston, 1920). Criticism occurred because the YMCA charged for its wares. Soldiers complained that a five-cent package of spearmint gum cost ten cents at a YMCA canteen. Another problem for the YMCA perhaps was its employment of socially prominent men as field officials, whereas the Salvation Army sent people with backgrounds akin to those of the troops.

2. Sherwood refers obliquely to the miles of U.S. Army vehicles that caused a traffic jam during the St. Mihiel offensive. Premier Georges Clemenceau was caught in it when he sought to visit Thiaucourt and gained a poor opinion of the army's road discipline.

3. PC meant command post.

4. An OP was an observation post.

5. The *Stars and Stripes* was the AEF newspaper published in Paris.

6. Reference to opening of the battle of the Meuse-Argonne.

7. "Our band, Saxaphone Sextette and a few miscellaneous entertainers, put on a show last night at the Cinema, which was about the best that has been pulled yet. Chet Neff, of Indianapolis, can't be beat singing jazz songs and his comedy

stuff leading our famous Saxaphone Sextette sure is there. He could go big at any
vaudeville show, with his 'Wild, Wild Women' song, accompanied by the Sextette.
We also have a good tenor singer in John Vance of Indpls and the band is devel-
oping into a real concert organization. Cecil Webb, of Blgtn., put on a French
beauty makeup and got by better with it than Joe [Josephine] Baker used to. The
band gave a concert for the General from just outside our office window a day or
two ago—they keep pretty busy giving concerts at the hospitals and various little
towns around." William A. Seward to Edith Regester, June 19, 1918, Seward Papers,
42nd Division Survey, U.S. Army Military History Institute, Army War College,
Carlisle Barracks, Pa.

   8. "Parade rest" was a part of drill in which soldiers spread their feet and
presumably rested.

CHAPTER SEVEN

   1. Montfaucon was one of the attack's first objectives because its elevation
allowed a long-range view and hence a great opportunity for targeting. Delay in its
capture was part of the reason the American offensive bogged down.

   2. The 314th F.A. was part of the Thirtieth Division.

   3. Col. Robert Tyndall's escape was close. Closer still was that of two battalion
commanders. "While selecting battery positions yesterday, one of my majors had a
piece of paper knocked out of his hand by piece of shell, another major standing
next to me had a piece of shell scratch his neck but did not even mark the skin."
Robert Tyndall, letter to Dean Spellman Tyndall, Oct. 8, 1918, folder 3, box 2,
Robert H. Tyndall Collection, 1916–1943, M280, Indiana Historical Society,
Indianapolis. But it was too close for one of the colonel's men, a comrade of whom
wrote afterward: "At 3 I was awakened for guard, but I was so cold I did not get up.
I laid awake when Lt. Cliff came down and yelled for the guard about 3:45. I was
certainly a damn fool for doing such a thing. Never again. We got up at 9:30, had
mess, and then Johnson and I started digging our hole. We worked on it the rest
of the morning, and part of afternoon. The Germans were dropping shells all
around us, and at 3:30 a shell lit within 10 ft. of Johnson and my hole, killing him
and putting a very small hole in my leg. It also wounded Hayes, Vincent, Truax and
Ullikan. We went to first aid station, and the first three named were sent to the hospital. I came back and Menifer and I put up a tent and got the bed ready. My blankets are full of holes. Got to bed at 6:30, up at 9. Fired from 9:25 until 1 A.M. Got
to bed at 1:30." Ervin M. Johannes Diary, Oct. 8, 1918, Forty-second Division
Survey, U.S. Army Military History Institute, Army War College, Carlisle Barracks,
Pa. Evidently Johannes and Johnson received the task of digging a hole, a typical
punishment, because of failure to get up for guard duty.

   4. At full strength a U.S. Army division contained 28,000 men, and it was difficult for the troops to know exactly what was going on. In the present case,
Sherwood's analysis, his diary entries for October 14–16 missed the crucial engagement of the Rainbow's participation in the war. The two brigades of infantry on the
front line were both in serious trouble and suffered heavy casualties. On the left
the two regiments of the Eighty-third Brigade under Brig. Gen. Michael J. Lenihan
rushed heavily wired, impregnable position in the German line in front of the town
of Landres et St. Georges and accomplished nothing save to pile up hundreds of
dead and wounded. The wire was deeply staked several yards across and loosely
attached, making it difficult to cut. Cutting the wire with hand pliers forced the
men to be in the open for prolonged periods and made them easy targets for

machine gunners. Artillery was of no use. Several months earlier Col. George E. Leach of the 151st put five hundred rounds on twenty feet of wire (George E. Leach, *War Diary*, [Roanoke, Va.: National Association, Rainbow Division Veterans, 1962], 35 [Apr. 25, 1918], to no avail. Incidentally, the Fifth Corps commander, Maj. Gen. Charles P. Summerall, a former artillery brigade commander of the Forty-second Division, asked the 150th F.A. to put shell fire between Landres et St. Georges and the Côte, the hill, of Chatillon "in the field of wire" on this occasion, a surprising command. Undated message, Sixty-seventh F.A. Brig., G-3 memos, 1918, 32.15, box 35, Forty-second Division historical, entry 1241, RG 120, National Archives. The corps commander relieved Lenihan. On the right side of the line were the regiments of the Eighty-fourth Brigade under Gen. Douglas MacArthur, who when Summerall told him he wanted the Côte de Chatillon or six thousand casualties, the entire strength of the brigade, asserted that he would take Chatillon. Among the casualties would be the brigade commander. He was bluffing; the hill was as difficult as Landres et St. Georges. He had no idea how his men would take the hill. One of his recommendations was a bayonet charge at night, an impossibility, which his colonels vetoed. But on the sixteenth the two regiments of the Eighty-fourth, the one on the right the Iowa, the left the Alabamas, took the Côte de Chatillon. The hill was crucial to defense of the German main line in the Meuse-Argonne, the Kriemhilde Stellung. Its capture was a great victory and made MacArthur's reputation. The Forty-second's infantrymen, those who survived, were exhausted, indeed the entire First Army that attacked all along the line on October 14 was exhausted. Two weeks later, on November 1, the army, by that time under command of Maj. Gen. Hunter Liggett, attacked and routed the German divisions. Incidentally, Sherwood's description of tanks coming up also demonstrated his lack of understanding of what happened, for there were only a few and they were put out of action by German antitank guns or the mechanical breakdowns that plagued the light French-made Renaults.

   5. Generally the reverse of a hill was safe from plunging fire—shells had to continue their trajectories. The Germans, however, were skillful with machine guns and could threaten troops on a far side.

   6. The Lafayette Escadrille was the American squadron that fought for the French before American entry into the war.

   7. Sherwood evidently was "busted" when he loaded "Rabbits" into a railroad car and the horse was injured.

   8. It was on this date that Colonel Tyndall had another narrow escape. As he wrote his daughter, the reason he survived was that the German soldier who constructed his dugout did such a thorough job:

   "Dear Amy: I must tell you about my dugout home and my little friends who live with me. I inherited the roommates of the German who built this dugout. There are two fat rats that play around after my candle is out. Last night they had a footrace over me as I tried to sleep. Then there are some snails. In the candlelight their tails look like snakes. I decided to have a housecleaning, but gave it up when I found my little friends had so many separate rooms. Then besides they have about as much need for protection as I have and maybe they also have kiddies waiting for them someplace. There are some lively fleas that feed at night and flocks of cooties. There is just room for my cot and a stove in which I keep a fire continuously to keep us (rats, snails, fleas, cooties and myself) warm. We are almost below the water level. I back in and

crawl out. The shell that had my name on it, as the soldiers say, arrived today, and, strange as it may sound to you, I owe my life to a German, the one that built this dugout and made it so safe and strong. I was dreaming on my cot, a dream caused by the enemy bombardment, and my dream turned into a nightmare in which I was captured, and, thinking what a disgrace to be a prisoner and not even wounded, when I woke up and found I was lying on my back, buried in dirt from the top of my dugout. The entrance was filled with dirt and smoke. This was 3:30 a.m. A shell had hit directly over my cot. My post of command was smashed like a house of cards. The Germans are determined to make me walk, too, as my favorite horse was wounded in three places by shell fragments and my automobile was hit again, and the enemy is still shelling while I write to you by candlelight, and the town, about one hundred yards from me, is sounding gas alarms. (Gas goes down, you know, and my dugout is above the town, so I don't have to put on my mask this time.) A German aviator dropped a message for us which said, 'Come on over while the coming is good and surrender and stop the war.' We sent back, 'Yes, we're coming all right, but not the way you want us to.' Tell Sam [the colonel's little son] that his letter is to be all about balloons and airplanes. Where do you go so often? You always end your letters, 'I must go now.'"
Letter of Oct. 28, unidentified newspaper clipping, Elmer Sherwood Papers, Lilly Library, Indiana University, Bloomington, Ind.

9. "One year ago today our ship banged into France. One year ago today we saw land for the first time in two weeks. Today we are seeing what H-E shells can do to the same land. Lord, what the things that have happened in that year! These months of it in a training camp learning how to fight the Boche and the remaining nine months putting our training into practice. We've sure done our share of practicing. Put on our two service stripes today." Bruce E. Geelhoed, comp. and ed., "The Kniptash Diaries, 1917–1919" (unpublished manuscript, Ball State University, 1999), Oct. 31.

10. "Got up for guard at 1. At 2:30 they woke up the rest of the fellows so that they could dress full. At 3 we laid the pieces, and at 3:30 the big barrage began. The noise was awful. There were a lot of machine gun bullets around here, and one set the second section powder dump on fire. We started with #3 charge, and ended with double 00. About 10, I got too close, and got knocked out by the piece. I came to about 12:30. Went to sleep about 3. Got 3 letters from Violet." Johannes diary, Nov. 1.

11. Seventeenth F.A. Regiment, Second Division.

12. Sherwood was wrong; the French accepted the city's surrender. Artillery of the Forty-second meanwhile placed the double-tracked railroad under fire.

13. Probably the experience of Battery B was similar to that of Battery F: "Our pathology was that of a man waking from a terrible dream and not being able to free himself immediately from the horror of it. It was not until darkness fell that we came to a realization that the war was over, as far as active hostilities were concerned. The full meaning of 'The Day,' as we always referred to the date when the armistice was signed, was flashed upon us in the flickering lights of hundreds of open campfires and in the dancing lights from hundreds of rockets and flares which were sent up that night in celebration of the event." Paul L. Palmerton, ed., *Under the Rainbow: Battery F, 150th F.A.* (Indianapolis: The Battery, 1919), 30.

CHAPTER EIGHT

1. The *Paris Herald.*

2. As the German troops advanced into Belgium the populace resisted through ambushes and sniper attacks on the Germans. The Germans took hostages at random, and during the 1914 invasion there were arbitrary executions. The woman's story, however, is unbelievable.

3. The Belgian language would have been Flemish. American engineer Herbert Hoover in 1914 organized a Belgian relief effort that passed food through the Allied blockade, which was paid for by private individuals and the U.S. government.

4. Again a story that does not ring true.

5. Sherwood was writing of the city of Luxembourg, to be sure.

6. "Well, we did it, and we're here, all of us, sore feet and all. The hike easily covered 40 kil. And it was up and downhill all the way. They call this little strip of country we just passed thru 'Little Switzerland.' Suppose it's because of its mountainous terrain. If the Alps are any worse than these hills then I don't want to get anywhere near them. I think we climbed a thousand hills today, and I don't remember any of them having an 'other side.' Don't remember going down a hill, it was always up. We must be a million miles above sea level. We start at 7:30 A.M. and reach this town of Rosport at 5:00 P.M. It was steady going all the time. Rested for a half hour at noon to eat a corn willy sandwich and rested about five minutes every 10 kilometers." E. Bruce Geelhoed, comp. and ed., "The Kniptash Diaries, 1917–1919" (unpublished manuscript, Ball State University, 1999), Dec. 2.

7. Prince Albert tobacco.

8. "After 8 straight days of hiking (12 to 40 kilos a day), we are halted for a couple days rest, and have our headquarters in Kerpen (Germany) in the old (1100 and something) castle of Baron Fritz von Wille, which is on the highest peak around and is some place. The place is a mass of ruins around the outside, and the main part seems to be a remodeling of the old joint and is finished up fine on the inside with old furniture, relics, chandeliers, etc. The old Baron is quite a painter and has some fine oil, etc. paintings, which are good. He isn't around now, but has an attendant here who jumps around and fixes up everything. The view from the tower is very beautiful. There is a concealed trapdoor in the room where our office is, leading down into a wine cellar, but the one we stole from Capt. Moore was huckleberry jam, so couldn't celebrate tonight. The wall in our office room is covered with a big painting extending all around. Some place to put in a birthday, but, of course, Bloomington would be better." William A. Seward to Edith Regester, Dec. 9, 1918, Seward Papers, Forty-second Division Survey, U.S. Army Military History Institute, Army War College, Carlisle Barracks, Pa.

CHAPTER NINE

1. He perhaps exaggerated the number of tunnels.

2. "I will now endeavor to tell you about the town we are stationed in now, as it is some place so good we wonder how we got it. It is the French Lick or Centerville of Germany and is simply a hotel town—streets of fine hotels, bathhouses and shops. We have our headquarters in the best hotel in town, and have our office in the big coffee room, next to the street, which is some room—electric and gas lights, gas grate, rug, divan, fine tables, chairs, big windows, curtains, etc.—extra good for a civilian room." William A. Seward to Edith Regester, Dec. 19, 1918, Seward Papers, Forty-second Division Survey, U.S. Army Military History Institute, Army War

College, Carlisle Barracks, Pa. Martinsville, twenty miles above Bloomington, contained a part known as Centerville, with hotels that offered mineral baths. The testimony of Vernon E. Kniptash was similar: "Started hiking at 9:00 A.M. on our final hike. Passed thru several towns that were used as summer resorts. Beautiful places. Looked very American. After 20 kil. of heavy hiking we reached this town of Bad Neuenahr. It's like Wonderland. The buildings are gay; the people are gay; everything is gay. Every other building is a hotel. Large hotels too. It's a summer resort for English, French and all countries. That is, it was before the war. We are quartered in a big hotel and have set up station. Feather beds, running water, electric lights, and in fact, all modern conveniences. It's too much. I just naturally yelled when I saw what we would have to put up with. After sleeping in hog pens, gutters, etc. for a year and then finally be billeted in a place like this. Again I say, it's too much. And there's only 5 candy stores in town. Sure as Hell I bought 25 marks worth." E. Bruce Geelhoed, comp. and ed., "The Kniptash Diaries, 1917–1919" (unpublished manuscript, Ball State University, 1999), Dec. 16, 1918. "Regt. Sure hit lucky when we drew the town. We're living better than Div. H.Q. The higher-ups didn't know at the time they were assigning us towns, just what sort of place Neuenahr was or we'd have never got within a hundred miles of it. I'm still afraid they'll rank us out." Ibid., Jan. 18, 1919.

3. "We are having a regular parade war now, and, after getting out of all such rigmarole while we were in the States and during the war, I have to carry the flag and wrestle with them all now. Day before yesterday we had a practice review by the Colonel, and yesterday we had a big review and minute inspection by Maj. General [C.A.F.] Flagler, Division Commander, which brought consternation right down on us. Everyone forgot all the war, and, of course, there were numerous 'ball-ups,' but everyone made them, so couldn't lay the blame on anyone. This afternoon we had a parade and ceremony in honor of Ex-Pres. Roosevelt, whose death we learned of yesterday, so we will be all paraded up by the time we get home." Seward to Regester, Jan. 1919, Seward Papers.

4. "For the past three days we've been posing for photographs. One day a picture of the whole Regiment. The next day a picture of the H.Q. Col. It's getting tiresome. Hope they get one to suit them. Guess Bob [Col. Robert H. Tyndall] wants to have something to show the folks when [he] gets back. 'Me and my regiment.'" Geelhoed, comp. and ed., "Kniptash Diaries," Jan. 16, 1919.

CHAPTER TEN

1. At this time the influenza epidemic was at its height. "It is pretty tough for my regiment to lose twelve men from disease in two weeks when I had only lost eleven other cases thru disease in eighteen months before that time, but the 'flu' has hit the Third Army pretty hard." Robert Tyndall to Dean [Spellman Tyndall], Mar. 7, 1919, folder 10, box 2, Robert H. Tyndall Collection, 1916–1943, M280, Indiana Historical Society, Indianapolis.

2. A hut was the World War I word for a Y building.

CHAPTER ELEVEN

1. The Knights of Columbus offered reading rooms, stationery, and other amenities.

2. Segregation of African Americans took place in both World Wars.

3. The painting Sherwood refers to is by Paul Chabas (1912) of a woman bathing at sunrise.

4. *Prisoniers de guerre.*

CHAPTER TWELVE

1. Robert Tyndall was suffering from influenza. Services of Supply, the AEF's supply organization.

2. The phrase he objected to had appeared in magazines and newspapers.

3. Pershing reviewed the divisions of the AEF, one after the other, and very few of the men enjoyed the experience. The reviewing doubtless made the C. in C. feel good and had the additional result of keeping the men busy. "Well the job is done, and we'll now kneel and give thanks. Sunday morn, and we got up at 6:00 A.M. Hiked up to a big field, a little piece out of Remagen, and got there at 11:00 A.M. Found out that the Review would start at 1:00 P.M. Nothing to do but stand around and wait for his Majesty. He showed up at 1:40. Only 40 minutes late. [Pershing was notoriously late for appointments.] Pretty good for a man of his rank. He started the inspection immediately. There was something like 30,000 men on that field. Never knew there was so many soldiers in the world. No wonder we won the war. Jack must have walked 15 kil. to inspect that gang. After the inspection, he pinned medals on the different men and officers that were recommended for them. Sgt. Murphy of A. Battery got one. Was mighty glad to see him get it, as the whole world knows he earned it. He kept on firing his piece when a whole box of powder charges were burning around him. Then the whole Division passed in review. It's quite some sight to see 30,000 men marching at one time. There wasn't a hitch at any time. Then Pershing made a speech to us. We highballed home in trucks. Got home at 6:00 P.M. That made 12 solid hours of standing on our feet. I was sure a tired soldier." E. Bruce Geelhoed, comp. and ed., "The Kniptash Diaries, 1917–1919" (unpublished manuscript, Ball State University, 1999), Mar. 16. Well-known playwright Charles G. MacArthur, a private in the 149th, remembered the speech: "All would have been well if he hadn't tried to make a la-de-da Y.M.C.A. speech after the inspection was all over. There were many newspapermen present, and he probably had to say Something of the Right Nature. So in thin, carrying tones he proceeded to speak of our Women Folks at Home, how glorious, sacred, and sainted they were, how vital it was that we return to them with the same purity and high ideals that made our hearts so many little gardens during the war. Right here rude noises began to arise from the Kansas contingent, together with much shooshing by officers. Pershing smelled a mouse and did a hurried right-about-face, fairly shouting that he was PROUD to meet this SPLEN-did division whose GLOR-ious rec-ORD had caught the imagin-ATION of the world. There was no more talk of what a young man of twenty-five ought to know." *War Bugs* (Garden City, N.Y.: Doubleday, Doran, 1929), 285.

4. M.G. meant machine gun. The 149th and 151st seem to have had more attention than the 150th, presumably because they still had horses. Col. George E. Leach was proud of the appearance of his regiment: "The General made a detailed inspection of the horses and material. He was very complimentary to the 151st F. A. When we marched out to our position, where we were to be inspected, we took along all our cleaning material with us. The horses were all groomed again, the carriages washed and the hoofs of the horses painted black, and they made a fine appearance." George E. Leach, *War Diary* (Roanoke, Va.: National Association, Rainbow Division Veterans, 1962), 104 (Mar. 17, 1919).

5. "This evening we pulled away from here. Don't give a damn if I ever see this country again." Ervin M. Johannes Diary, Apr. 18, Forty-second Division Survey, U.S. Army Military History Institute, Army War College, Carlisle Barracks, Pa.

6. Capacity of the *Leviathan* was twelve thousand.

7. The men deeply resented the army's caste system. Weeks earlier, while the regiment was in Germany, Vernon E. Kniptash had a taste of it. "Last day of February, and also the last day of school. Hung around the 'Y' all afternoon and night. Saw moving pictures of the 'Salt of the Earth.' Was coming back to the billets happy and on good terms with the whole world when I passed the officers' quarters and then things changed. The officers and nurses and Y.M.C.A. women and things were having a dance. I looked in the window, and the 'scenery' gave me the Blues so bad I had to leave. Hall was beautifully decorated, and a big Jazz Band and these birds trotted around having a glorious time. It hurt. However these American women over here are officers' meat, and their meat only. We've been fighting for Democracy for a year and yet it's a court-martial for the enlisted men caught talking to one of these dear things. I used to think it was an honorable thing for a woman to come over here and do war work, but I've found out lots of things since then. The old Sam Browne belt can work wonders. I know lots and lots of officers that are men, but I know a whole lot more that are _____. Well, in a couple of months things are going to even up a bit. It's going to take more than a Sam Browne to get by. Heard a good story this eve. A couple of enlisted men were walking down the street and cross the paths of a couple of nurses. The nurses said, 'Hello boys.' One of the men turned around and said, 'I beg your pardon miss, but you must be mistaken, we're not officers.' It sure took a fall out of the old girl. She exited like a clam. Lord, I'll be glad when the day comes that I can tell some of these birds to go to Hell. They might as well be overbearing while they can because it won't work in civvies. . . . Just been reading over all that I've written tonight, and it sounds like jealousy on my part. It isn't jealousy. It's the unfairness of everything to the enlisted men. He hasn't got a chance." Geelhoed, comp. and ed., "Kniptash Diaries," Feb. 28. The Sam Browne belt was a British concoction, invented for officers of the Indian Army and adopted by the AEF.

8. American Library Association.

9. Floyd Gibbons, a prominent journalist in the 1920s with the *Chicago Tribune*, was with the Second Division at Belleau Wood, near Château-Thierry, and was shot in the eye. His eye patch added to his fame.

10. Sherwood's diary missed the excitement in New York harbor: "Tugs from the different States came out to greet respective Regiments. Indiana had two tugs, and we're well represented on a third. The boys finally cut loose, and the din was awful. Miss Liberty loomed into sight, and that coupled with those tug boats full of Hoosiers was too much for the boys. I'll frankly say that big tears came to my eyes, and I wasn't ashamed because everybody else was affected the same. Then somebody let out a blood-curdling yell, and that acted like a cork out of a bottle for all. Everybody went wild, dancing, sparring, yelling, and kissing. Lord knows what not. A bunch of raving maniacs. I feel as hysterical as a damned old woman. The tugs followed us till we were ready to turn into our piers, and then they had to leave. We were all chased down below after that. Geelhoed, comp. and ed., "Kniptash Diaries," Apr. 25.

11. *Indianapolis Star.*

Further Reading

The materials about World War I are large and might seem more than a reader would care to encounter, but they are manageable because American participation lasted a year and a half and almost all fighting took place after April 1918—the first American divisions entered the line earlier only for training. By far the largest engagement was the Meuse-Argonne, which began September 26 and ended with the armistice, November 11.

The best sources of information, the place to start, are Pershing's memoirs together with those of his commanders, and for the war department in Washington the memoirs of Gen. Peyton C. March, chief of staff beginning early in 1918, and of his assistants. It is important to include both Pershing's subordinates and officers at home for they made possible the creation of the army in France. Because of the dominant personality of the AEF's commander-in-chief it has been customary to give his activities undue attention in the way that students of the Civil War considered Grant and Lee. For general accounts see Russell F. Weigley's history of the U.S. Army and his accompanying volume analyzing strategy and policy. Highly readable are the biographies, monographs, or edited works by Daniel R. Beaver, Larry I. Bland, Edward M. Coffman, James Lawton Collins, Jr., James A. Cooke, Harvey A. DeWeerd, James E. Hewes, Jr., D. Clayton James, Allan R. Millett, Timothy K. Nenninger, Forrest C. Pogue, Donald Smythe, and David F. Trask. For the 150th Field Artillery there is Elmer Frank Straub, *A Sergeant's Diary in the World War: The Diary of an Enlisted Member of the 150th Field Artillery (Forty-Second [Rainbow] Division)* (Indianapolis: Indiana Historical Bureau, 1923) and Paul L. Palmerton, ed., *Under the Rainbow: Battery F, 150th F.A., A History of Its Service in the War against Germany* (Indianapolis: Battery F, 1919), the latter the Bloomington battery. Phil Reyburn, "Letters from a World War I Soldier," *Indiana Military History Journal* 2 (Jan. 1977): 5–14, is a selection of Sherwood's letters together with his shipboard diary en route to France. Hazel E. Crawford, "Indiana's Victory Celebration of World War I," ibid. 4 (Oct. 1979): 16–19, describes the 150th's reception in Indianapolis.

The present book has used personal papers, for which see especially the letters and diary of William A. Seward (42nd Division survey, U.S. Army Military History Institute, Army War College, Carlisle Barracks, Pennsylvania) and for an introduction Jennifer Wagner, "For Home and Country," *Indiana Alumni Magazine* 62 (2000): 34–36. See also the Ervin M. Johannes diary (42nd Division survey, MHI). Much worth reading is the diary of Vernon E. Kniptash, compiled and edited by E. Bruce Geelhoed of Ball State University, Muncie, Indiana. The David H. Ramsay diary is in the Lilly Library of Indiana University, Bloomington. Robert H. Tyndall's papers (Indiana Historical Society, Indianapolis) contain detailed letters to his wife and a short diary. Two collections in the Indiana State Library proved of little use, the Norman B. Nash papers offering a chaplain's details of deaths and burials, and the Frank W. Buschmann papers documenting the captain's service.

A reader may wish to search out the history of the other two regiments of Sherwood's artillery brigade, the 149th or 151st, or perhaps even the history of the 42nd Division. For the brigade there is Charles G. MacArthur, *A Bug's-Eye View of the War* (n.p.: 1919), the Illinois regiment (149th), republished as *War Bugs* (Garden City, N.Y.: Doubleday, Doran, 1929), and for the Minnesota regiment Louis L. Collins, *History of the 151st Field Artillery, Rainbow Division* (St. Paul: Minnesota War Commission, 1929), and the diary of its colonel, George E. Leach, published privately in 1923, reprinted as *War Diary* (Roanoke, Va.: Rainbow Division Veterans, 1962). A recent divisional history is James J. Cooke, *The Rainbow Division in the Great War* (Westport, Conn.: Praeger, 1994). Worth reading is the detailed account by the commander of the Rainbow's 83rd Infantry Brigade, Henry J. Reilly, *Americans All: The Rainbow at War: Official History of the 42nd Rainbow Division in the War* (Columbus, Ohio: Heer, 1936). Each of the four infantry regiments sponsored a history. The Rainbow Division inspired a large number of memoirs, for which see the Reilly volume.

Index